ASPECTS OF
NORTHERN LINCOLNSHIRE

ASPECTS *of*
NORTHERN
LINCOLNSHIRE

Edited by
Jenny Walton

Series editor
Brian Elliott

Wharncliffe Books

First Published in 2002 by
Wharncliffe Books
an imprint of
Pen and Sword Books Limited,
47 Church Street, Barnsley,
South Yorkshire. S70 2AS

*For up-to-date information on other titles produced under the
Wharncliffe imprint, please telephone or write to:*

> Wharncliffe Books
> FREEPOST
> 47 Church Street
> Barnsley
> South Yorkshire S70 2BR
> Telephone (24 hours): 01226 - 734555

ISBN: 1-903425-17-4

A CIP catalogue record of this book is available from the
British Library

Cover illustration: *from a painting by David Waller, Woodhall Spa, entitled: 'Another Day', courtesy of Primetime Video
Productions, Eastville, Boston who have copyright on the prints.*
Contents page illustration: *Sea Bank Road, 1902, before construction of the Kingsway promenade in 1906. Courtesy
of Grimsby Central Library.*

Printed in the United Kingdom by
CPI UK

CONTENTS

INTRODUCTION

by Jenny Walton

When it was decided to produce a book in the *Aspects* series relating to Lincolnshire, the first decision that had to be made was – which part of Lincolnshire? After all, as one of the largest counties in the country, there is so much to offer a local historian that the area obviously would have to be divided up for the sake of this particular type of publication.

For this reason, we are looking at the northern area of Lincolnshire in this book – that is, the approximate region covered by the North Lincolnshire and North East Lincolnshire Councils (the whole having been known as South Humberside before boundary changes in April 1996), as well as dipping over the border into the northernmost reaches of Lincolnshire County Council. After all, to most people, regardless of any Authority boundary changes, 'it's always been all Lincolnshire, anyway'. This may make for some perplexing reading as, within the chapters, you will find references to 'Lincolnshire' – meaning the contemporary county (Chapter 1, for example), whilst 'north Lincolnshire', when referred to in Chapter 2, actually relates to the northern area of Lincolnshire (as covered in this book), and not to 'North Lincolnshire', the region covered by the unitary authority of that name.

I have included a map of the area covered in *Aspects of Northern Lincolnshire* so that those of you unfamiliar with the region may find your way around. Opposite the map is a poem, written by John Malvert, whose words aptly describe the northern Lincolnshire shoreline.

The whole of northern Lincolnshire is an area of great beauty, with few towns and no cities. Contrary to that which most of the rest of the nation believes, its topography is not really 'flat' at all, and its Wolds are widely recognised as being an area of great beauty. The region is mainly agricultural, with picturesque market towns and villages scattered everywhere – some of which are so small that, if you blink as you drive past, you may miss them.

Grimsby (happily and justly promoting itself as Europe's food town), and Scunthorpe, the town that arose from steel-making, are the main urban areas and again, it must be pointed out, however, that, regardless of what comedians may say, these are not grubby industrialised sprawls but attractive places where trees, grassland, parks and colourful flower beds abound – both on routes leading into, and within, their busy developments. The main industrial concerns, for which Northern Lincolnshire is renowned, are based alongside the Humber bank, the region's natural northernmost boundary, with further pockets of carefully controlled Business Parks and Industrial Estates sited strategically around the area.

This is a region that has a history going back for thousands of years, as Edward Dickinson explains in the opening chapter. Because of the wealth of material from which to draw, he has limited his contribution to cover the area now known as North East Lincolnshire, before the Iron Age, illustrating it with examples of finds that give an insight of its inhabitants at that time.

It is a well known fact that local history is a subject studied by thousands, its popularity increasing all the time as people delve into their own family and locale's origins. This is a relatively new phenomenon as, once, few non-professional historians had the time, education and financial ability to study the subject. But it is thanks to these early researchers that we, their modern counterparts, have some written records to use as stepping stones into whatever branch of local history may interest us. Nick Lyons, in Chapter 2, has made some of these past historians – themselves now a part of local history lore – a subject of his own research. From the eighteenth/nineteenth century and de la Pryme (he of the fascinating Diary), into the early twentieth century, including the perhaps lesser-known beings such as Oliver, Poulson and Ball, Nick has brought them to life for the reader.

Richard Clarke takes us in a completely different direction (pardon the pun) with his description of a contemporary walk along the Clay Bank, that man-made clay, or reinforced, bank on the south shore of the River Humber. The route he describes leads from Cleethorpes at the mouth of the River Humber, to the mouth of the River Trent at its head. He highlights various geographical, environmental and man-made structures as part of the walk's changing scenery and where, from all points, Yorkshire, on the opposite bank of the Humber, is visible. It is a walk that Richard would like to see made official and publicised, so that more people will know about, and enjoy it.

On a completely different tack, Kevin Gracie's chapter describes the version of Grimsby's origins as researched by himself and other members of the Grim and Havelock Association. Within this work, he reveals the discovery of important, previously overlooked evidence that helps endorse the Association's claims for the legend having actually been based on fact. Readers will note that some chapters contain cross-references – for example, 'Ye Byrde of Gryme' of Kevin's piece is also referred to by Oliver, one of Nick Lyons' historians. Later, de la Pryme also turns up in Chapter 6.

Whilst studying for her degree in English literature and History, Karen Prescott discovered the existence of the Humber keels and the great part they played in our nation's history, especially from the eighteenth to the early twentieth centuries. Now that there are so very few left in existence, she felt inspired to write about them – especially for the sakes of all those who know little or nothing about such craft ('...usually people below the approximate age of forty-five,' she says).

Ray Carey's detailed research into the drainage of the Ancholme Valley during the seventeenth century has led him to produce a fascinating account of the building of South Ferriby's Great Sluice – a tremendous, although controversial, achievement.

The famous and thriving Cleethorpes is the subject of the next two chapters, by Alan Dowling and Joanne Mason respectively. Both concern Cleethorpes as a holiday resort and complement each other. Alan gives us a detailed picture of the promenades and the changes that their construction made to the town, especially its roadways, whilst Joanne has produced a general overview of Cleethorpes' rise to fame, from the development of the foreshore through to different types of entertainment seen there over the hundred and fifty or so years since it became popular. Both authors have illustrated their work with old photographs, and it is fascinating to compare the same, but changing, scenes caught forever in different periods of time.

I was fortunate enough to be introduced to a gentleman who lived from the mid-eighteenth century until well into the nineteenth century. Although it may be a moot point as to whether or not he is aware of me, I have learned a lot about him through his letters to his family in Hull and northern Lincolnshire. In fact, he and his way of life have so enthralled me that I am now involved in further research about the man and his times with the intention of producing a book about him. I am only sorry that the sudden demise of Ron Short, the descendant of that seaman, and the one who originally lent me these letters, has meant he cannot see the chapter in print, nor know of the latest developments of my research. Always so full of enthusiasm for the subject, he would have been delighted.

Another piece of ancestral memorabilia led to Neil Wilkyn's chapter on pre-enclosure farming in Barrow-upon-Humber.

Researching his family tree, he came across paperwork written by farming relatives who lived during the eighteenth century. He shares with us some of the intriguing facts he has discovered about farm life, stock prices, workers' wages and general daily life. It really does set a wonderful example for us all, reminding us that we should take time to personally record our own daily lives, no matter how mundane they may seem – who knows what pleasure and educational benefits they will bring our own descendants?

The contents of the penultimate chapter were a must for the book. Lincolnshire was, and is still known as, 'Bomber County' – so it is only natural that we should cover the subject of Second World War airfields and their importance. Patrick Otter, who has researched the subject thoroughly and is widely respected for his knowledge, was the obvious and best person to write this for us.

Finally, with the help of Garry Crossland of ABP, Grimsby, I have put together a very brief history of Grimsby's fishing heritage. There were so many stories of bravery, penury and determination, along with reams of facts and figures, within those many documents and books available to the interested reader, that I found the most difficult part of researching this fascinating subject was actually finding the willpower to stop – leaving me with a mere 30,000 or so words to précis into a final chapter for the book.

It has been a pleasure to handle the work of all the contributors to *Aspects of Northern Lincolnshire*; their enjoyment of and enthusiasm for their respective subjects has been only too obvious and I thank them for sharing their knowledge and beliefs with us all. If you, too, find the various subjects interesting, I shall be pleased to hear from you and will pass your comments on to the appropriate author.

Thanks must be given to David Waller who allowed us to use a copy of his painting, *Another Day*, one of a pair (the other is *Harvest Home*), as a front cover for the book, and to Primetime Video Productions, Eastville, Boston, who have the rights to the prints. Thank you, also, Brian Elliott, Series Editor, and the rest of the team at Wharncliffe, who have been so supportive and helpful during the compilation and editing of this publication.

Should you feel you could contribute a chapter of your own to another book in the Lincolnshire *Aspects* series, please contact: Jenny Walton, Editor, c/o Wharncliffe Books, 47 Church Street, Barnsley, S70 2AS, enclosing a brief description of the proposed article.

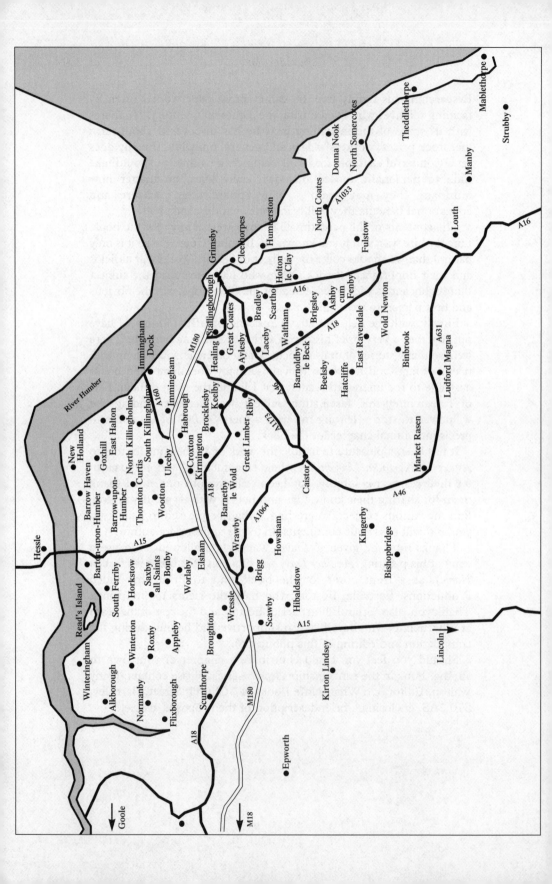

Pixel of a Coastline

John Malvert

The tide is on the turn.
Across the wind-blown flats
far water moves,
insinuating seawards.

•

Picked over by parading gulls,
static tide-mark waits to wash.
Dying life-force
seeks rejuvenation.

•

Sea edge of lazy water,
slow expanding waves
crisscross paths,
where granulated pebbles grind.

•

Small rivulets of water
channel light furrows,
as footmarks tramline behind a man and dog.

•

The burning sand reflects light,
disturbing vision.
Shimmering
heat rises up, on static air.

•

The sand-sifted grasses
break the colour-tone of dunes.
Worm casts stand proud
on wet, wave-patterned sand.

•

Toes encrusted with sand,
will wash at the ocean's edge.
Pervading thoughts –
mind imagines Lorelie[1].

1. Lorelei – from Germanic mythology: a siren of the Rhine whose singing lures sailors to shipwreck.

1. NORTH EAST LINCOLNSHIRE BEFORE THE IRON AGE

by J Edward Dickinson

THE INTENTION OF THIS CHAPTER is to provide a brief overview of the pre-Iron Age archaeology found within the Unitary Authority of North East Lincolnshire. It is not meant to be an exhaustive inventory of every prehistoric findspot, cropmark or earthwork in the Borough, nor is it meant to be a guide to the highlights, but a look at a representative sample. However, evidence for the earliest periods is restricted to a mere handful of sites, compared with dozens in the Bronze Age.

North East Lincolnshire Council came into being with the disaggregation of the former county of Humberside. It is made up of the towns of Grimsby, Cleethorpes and Immingham, and the surrounding countryside, from Habrough in the north to wold Newton in the south and Beelsby in the west. Geographically, the area consists of parts of the Lincolnshire Wolds and the Lincolnshire Marsh.

The Lincolnshire Wolds are a belt of chalk upland, up to fifteen kilometres wide and about seventy kilometres long, running north-west to south-east. The chalk escarpment is best developed in the central region to the south of Grimsby, where it is dissected by many streams such as the Waithe Beck. Here the Wolds reach a height of 168 metres above sea level. They slope eastwards to the Lincolnshire Marsh, a coastal plain divided into the Middle Marsh and the Outmarsh. The Middle Marsh consists of glacial till with areas of glacial sands and gravels overlaying the chalk; these are interspersed with gravel and sand left by numerous stream valleys, both past and present. The Middle Marsh is gently undulating between ten and twenty-five metres above sea level. To the east of this is the Outmarsh, a flat strip of alluvium below ten metres above sea level.

The last ten years has seen an increase in knowledge of the earliest human occupation in North East Lincolnshire. For example, in 1990 the area was believed initially to have been settled in the Neolithic or New Stone Age, but by 2002 there is definite evidence for occupation in the Mesolithic or Middle Stone Age and possible evidence of activity in the Palaeolithic or Old Stone Age.

Earliest evidence
The Palaeolithic was an extremely long period of hunter-gatherers, extending from the time when humans first evolved up to about 10,000 BC. In Britain, the earliest evidence of human activity dates from about 450,000 years ago, although there are long periods of 100,000 years or more when there appears to have been no human presence. The Palaeolithic is known to have experienced at least three major Ice Ages, when ice sheets, making most of the country unsuitable for human habitation, covered northern Britain. However, there were warm, or even hot periods, when hunter-gatherers would have lived in the region. The nomadic life-style of these people would have meant living in temporary camps, no traces of which survive in North East Lincolnshire. During one of these warmer periods, the Hoxnian interglacial, which occurred between 423,000 and 38,000 years ago, flint tools were deposited by Homo Neanderthalensis, Neanderthal Man, at Kirmington,[1] (North Lincolnshire). The only evidence for any Palaeolithic occupation within North East Lincolnshire is the recent discovery of a possible Lower Palaeolithic hand axe near the River Freshney at Laceby.

With the advent of modern humans around 40,000 years ago came the Upper Palaeolithic. This period was followed by the Mesolithic at of the end of the last Ice Age, around 10,000 BC. The Mesolithic, the last part of the hunter-gatherer time, can be seen as a bridge between the Old Stone Age and the New and is characterised by the emergence of sophisticated groups of hunter-gatherers. These people used spears and harpoons that incorporated very small sharp blades called microliths.

One such group may have camped near Grimsby at Pyewipe. A collection of material was retrieved from the upper reaches of the inter-tidal zone, in a small area of scrubby salt marsh developed on land in front of the sea defences. Paul Greenwood, the local archaeologist who discovered the site, has a collection of over 600 flints from there – mostly knapping debris, the material left over from producing flint tools. It includes unmodified chunks of flint, presumably put on one side to work on later, the core that the flint is chipped away from in the form of flakes, and the flakes themselves. The assemblage also includes a quantity of the tools made in this process, such as scrapers and microliths. Additionally, some of the flakes were retouched to produce a

Figure 1. A selection of Mesolithic flints from Pyewipe, near Grimsby.
Courtesy of the Humber Wetlands Project

useful tool (Figure 1).

With the end of the Mesolithic, approximately 4500 BC, came the Neolithic period, with changes so radical and important in the way people lived, that it is often referred to as the Neolithic Revolution. Amongst the many innovations was the use of pottery and monument building – indeed Stonehenge was begun in this period. But, without doubt, the most significant introduction was the domestication of plants and animals. Hunter-gathering no longer being the principle way of obtaining food in Britain, a settled pastoral lifestyle began to develop.

Like the Mesolithic, much of the evidence for human occupation in North East Lincolnshire comes from chance finds of flint tools and the waste material created in their production. However, there is also evidence of monuments people built and used. In the parish of

Beelsby, right on the boundary with Swallow village in Lincolnshire, is a large spinney: Ash Holt. Within it is a long irregular mound, some twenty-six metres in length and between five and sixteen metres wide, aligned south-west to north-east. This is a Neolithic long barrow. Standing at the upper end of a small valley running down to the Croxby and Waithe Becks, and seventy-six metres above sea level, the long barrow would have occupied a prominent position in the landscape.

The Ash Holt long barrow is the oldest surviving field monument in North Eastern Lincolnshire dating to between 3400 and 2400 BC. It is a funerary monument representing the burial place of the first farmers in the area and, like other long barrows, was probably used for communal burial with only parts of the human remains selected for interment. In other parts of the country, where other long barrows have been excavated, evidence shows their enclosures were clearly in use for a very long time. It is likely, therefore, that the Ash Holt long barrow, the most northerly of a group of long barrows along the valley of the Waithe Beck, acted as an important spiritual focus for the local community over a considerable period of time. Indeed the presence of the mound influenced the landscape into the medieval period, with the otherwise straight parish boundary between Swallow and Beelsby diverting around it to ensure it would be enclosed within Lincolnshire.

The long barrow survives well, its wooded location having served to protect it from ploughing over the centuries. However, small-scale quarrying has caused some damage to the southern end. This high degree of survival and archaeological significance was officially recognised in 1934 when it was placed on the *Schedule of Ancient Monuments*.

Further evidence for Neolithic occupation and burial practice in North East Lincolnshire was revealed at the Central Market National School, in Grimsby. This building stood at the corner of present day Market Street and King Edward Street, just to the east of Victoria Street North. During alterations at the end of the nineteenth century, workmen uncovered a wooden cyst or container.

When found it was about three feet in length, but exposure to the air has rendered it very friable. It is now in several pieces. It is a rude 'dugout', and it had been roughly hewn out of a portion of the trunk of an oak tree.[2]

The cyst contained ashes. Whether this was an isolated burial or associated with a long barrow is unknown.

There has been no excavation or archaeological survey of a Neolithic site in North East Lincolnshire. The other evidence of Neolithic occupation in the region comes from chance or stray finds of stone tools, flakes or cores – for example, a Neolithic flake found during digging for gravel in Wold Newton in 1828. The Reverend G Oliver became involved in the recovery of archaeological material when an Anglo-Saxon cremation cemetery, containing more than twenty urns, was discovered during the excavation of the gravel mound. It was he who discovered the small flint flake, which is now in the British Museum. Without Reverend Oliver's intervention, that flake would have been lost in the extracted gravel.

Two potential Neolithic settlements

Philip Wise, writing in 1990, commented that there was little evidence for settlement in the Neolithic period in the region, but he did identify two potential sites. The first, in the parish of Laceby, is close to the River Freshney. Here, two flint scrapers, normally used in the process of dressing and curing hide, were found. Alongside these were a few sherds, or pieces, of possibly Neolithic pottery and a perforated bone pin. Such finds are normally regarded as typical of a settlement site. At the second site, also by the Freshney but nearer to the coast at Little Coates, a similar selection of objects was found including flakes and cores. These would suggest the inhabitants were making tools on site, for, as in the Mesolithic period, the readily available flint nodules in these small river valleys would have been used for everyday tools. Other finds from the Little Coates site, a leaf-shaped arrowhead and a plano-convex knife – a flint tool with a convex top and a flat base – suggest that the site dates to the end of the Neolithic period.

The most numerous type of Neolithic find from North East Lincolnshire is the ground stone or flint axe. These are very interesting as they demonstrate another Neolithic innovation: trade over long distances. Axes of good stone or flint were at a premium in Neolithic society, and were regarded as a valuable commodity to be traded far and wide. Likewise, a good axe would have made a suitable gift to be exchanged between groups or communities, signifying some form of agreement.

The two flint axes from the Cleethorpes area were probably made at Grimes Grave in Norfolk where flint mines were worked in the late Neolithic period. Miners would have dug for flint using antlers as picks, and shovels made from animal shoulder blades. Where quality flint was not available other stones were used, the most suitable being tough, fine grained igneous or metamorphic rock, which could be given a sharp edge. Axe factories have been identified in Britain and Ireland. Perhaps the most famous is at Great Langdale in the English Lake District. Axes made here are distributed throughout England, Wales and Northern Ireland. However, of some 500 axes found throughout the country, well over fifty per cent came from North East Lincolnshire; of the eight axes found on the coastal plain around Grimsby and Cleethorpes, four originated from Cumbria.

With the end of the Neolithic, around 2300 BC, metal first began to be widely used in Britain, possibly as a result of an increase in contact with Europe. Nevertheless, various types of stone, particularly flint, still remained very important long after metal became available. This was the Bronze Age, a long period conveniently divided by archaeologists into the Early Bronze Age (from 2300-1200 BC) and the Late Bronze Age (*c*.1200-700 BC). Like the Neolithic, the Bronze Age in North East Lincolnshire is typified by chance finds and monuments. Stone axes (Figure 2) and tools and round barrows from the Early Bronze Age, as well as the occasional bronze artefact are found. The Bronze Age is also the earliest period where sites have been archaeologically excavated in North East Lincolnshire.

Figure 2. Late Neolithic and Early Bronze Age Stone Axes from North East Lincolnshire. (Scale in centimetres).*Courtesy of the North East Lincolnshire Archaeology Service*

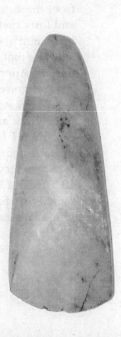

Figure 3. Collared funerary urn from the Bronze Age barrow at Bourne Lane, Grimsby. *Courtesy of the North East Lincolnshire Archaeology Service*

Round barrows are burial mounds dating from the Late Neolithic period to the Late Bronze Age, with examples mainly belonging to the period 2400-1500 BC. Their most prominent feature is the mound, with its construction dependant on the local geology. These mounds ranged in size from three metres to over sixty-five metres in diameter, and from about a half metre to over six metres in height. Most are only a roughly round shape; few are truly circular and, in Lincolnshire, frequently surrounded by a ditch. There are over 10,000 surviving round barrows recorded nationally and they are distributed across Lowland Britain.

Bronze Age Sites in Grimsby, an unsigned duplicated typescript, probably by R N Hannigan and dated November 1948, is held in the *North East Lincolnshire Sites and Monuments Record*. It describes archaeological work carried out at Bourne Lane, Grimsby, by L W Pye and R N Hannigan. A Bronze Age collared urn containing cremated bones and a bronze pin was recovered during the construction of F A Would Limited's new premises in Grimsby. When the site was subsequently inspected by Pye and Hannigan, they found that the urn (Figure 3) had come from the centre of a Bronze Age round barrow, between thirty-five and forty metres in diameter which, at the time, stood to a height of one metre above the ground surface. As with many round barrows, it appears that the Bourne Lane site was used for later, intrusive, burials. Approximately ten metres from the centre of the barrow another grave was found.

L W Pye was no stranger to excavating Bronze Age burial mounds. In 1935, he and T Sheppard partly excavated the Beacon Hill Bronze Age round barrow (Figure 4). This monument is on the south-western side of Cleethorpes cemetery, adjacent to the Second World War cemetery for merchant seamen. When excavated, the mound was 13.7 metres by 7.6 metres and three metres high. From it, a large number of finds were uncovered that are currently held by North East Lincolnshire Museums. A large undecorated urn, found in the

Figure 4. The 1930s excavation at Beacon Hill. *Courtesy of the North East Lincolnshire Archaeology Service*

centre of the mound, 1.8m below its surface, contained cremated remains, charcoal and four smaller urns (Figure 5). Each of the four smaller vessels, decorated with various patterns, contained the cremated remains of a child. Adjacent to the large urn containing these burials, there was another decorated urn, which also contained

Figure 5. Bronze Age pottery from Beacon Hill. *Courtesy of the North East Lincolnshire Archaeology Service*

the cremated remains of a child. Line drawings of these urns have been published.[2]

Whilst the urns are definitely of the Early Bronze Age period, Neolithic flints, including flakes, scrapers and cores have been found in the immediate vicinity of the Beacon Hill barrow. This, coupled with its shape, suggests that it may originally have been a Neolithic oval barrow with secondary Bronze Age use. The site continued to serve as a focal point into the medieval period, and was probably used for pagan Anglo-Saxon burials – as denoted by a possible item of grave goods, a small plain bowl found on the edge of the barrow. Such a prominent mound on the low ridge of a glacial moraine was ideal for the site of a beacon fire, a use documented in 1377, which gives the site its name.

Away from the coastal plain, on the higher ground of the Lincolnshire Wolds, is another fine Bronze Age round barrow. Situated at the top of a low rise overlooking the rear of Hatcliffe Manor House, this burial mound is slightly oval in shape – thirty metres by thirty-five metres – and stands about three metres high. It is gently rounded with a level top some nine metres in diameter. No evidence of a ditch is visible, but this could have silted up and filled in over time.

Despite having been long recognised as an antiquity, possibly forming a focus in the landscape ensemble of the formal gardens to the rear of Hatcliffe Manor, the round barrow appears undisturbed and has probably never been ploughed or excavated.

Both this round barrow and the one at Beacon Hill were designated as *Scheduled Ancient Monuments* in 2001.

Destroyed by the plough
Several other Bronze Age round barrows are known from North East Lincolnshire, but unfortunately most have been ploughed out over the millennia. They are now only visible as cropmarks in aerial photographs, where the disturbed ground causes the crop to grow at a different rate to the surrounding field. For example, a few hundred metres to the north of the Hatcliffe Manor round barrow, there are traces of a ring ditch, tentatively identified as the enclosure of a ploughed out round barrow.

A number of ploughed out Bronze Age round barrows can be more definitely identified. C W Phillips, working for the Ordnance Survey in the 1930s, described a round barrow in Hawerby-cum-Beesby as being 'a grass covered mound some 53 foot in diameter and 5 foot high'. Unfortunately, by 1963, the Ordnance Survey had to amend this to 'the feature had been almost levelled by ploughing'.[3] A recent visit by the North East Lincolnshire Council Archaeologist could find no trace of the round barrow.

Other possible round barrows are known to have been destroyed by development in the nineteenth and early twentieth centuries. For example, the Toothill area of Little Coates in Grimsby may have been the focus for several round barrows for, in 1904, when a mound was quarried there for sand, an urn and complete lower human jaw was recovered. Also, the Reverend G Oliver opened two barrows at Little Coates in 1825 and recovered a broken urn and human remains.[4]

Of those chance or stray finds from Early Bronze Age North East Lincolnshire, the most interesting is a stone axe-hammer found amongst the 'sunken forest' of Cleethorpes beach. Very much a chance find, it was in 1979 that Mr Shane Johnson was bait digging amongst the tree stumps when he unearthed the axe-hammer. Surprisingly, it still retained its haft, which unfortunately broke off and was lost at the time of its discovery.[5] However, the stump of the haft survived within the axe's perforation, allowing the wood to be identified as poplar. This unusual survival also meant that the axe-hammer could be dated scientifically at the Oxford Radiocarbon Accelerator Unit, showing the object was in use around 1400 BC.

Other Bronze Age stone implements have also been found throughout North East Lincolnshire, from a large polished stone axe found at West Ravendale, to the small barbed and tanged arrowhead from Ayelsby, and now in the North Lincolnshire Museum at Scunthorpe. A particularly attractive example of a Bronze Age barbed and tanged arrowhead was found outside North East Lincolnshire at Binbrook (Figure 6), but was donated to the then

Figure 6. Early Bronze Age arrowheads from Grimsby and Binbrook. (Scale in centimetres) *Courtesy of the North East Lincolnshire Archaeology Service*

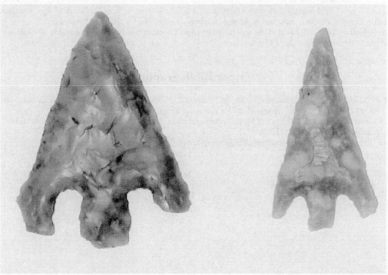

Great Grimsby Museum by W E R Hallgarth. It is now held by North East Lincolnshire Museums.

In addition to the Bronze Age stone tools, a small number of metal artefacts have been recovered. These include two bronze axe heads from Ashby-cum-Fenby. The smaller of the two is described as being 'socketed with a loop'. Such a small socketed axe would seem to be typical of the later Bronze Age, perhaps the eighth century. A Late Bronze Age date can also be ascribed to the other notable find of this period from North East Lincolnshire, a sword of the 'Ewart Park' type, found in Bradley. This object is also now at the North Lincolnshire Museum.

By the end of the Bronze Age, the climate had settled down and become similar to today's. North East Lincolnshire was an area of coastal marsh and peat, with settlement on the sand and gravel or till spurs and higher ground. The arrival of the Iron Age marks a distinct change in the known archaeology of the region, and is the era for which the first identifiable settlements are found and the first scientific excavation takes place.

This paper has sought to review the current state of knowledge of the pre-Iron Age periods in North East Lincolnshire. The pre Iron Age archaeology of the region is scarce and for several periods reliant on the evidence of only a handful of objects. For other periods, there are field monuments and possible landscapes. Unfortunately, no synthesis of the sites has been produced and no research carried out to place any of the findspots or monuments into their context.

Notes and References

1 J May (1976), *Prehistoric Lincolnshire*, p.82. History of Lincolnshire Committee, Lincoln.
2 J H Cooke (1898), 'Neolithic Life in Lincolnshire', *The Naturalist*, 221-4.
3 OS Card TF29 NE 1.
4 P J Wise (1990). The archaeology of the Grimsby-Cleethorpes area, in S. Ellis & D. R. Crowther (ed.), *Humber Perspectives: a region through the ages*, 213-26. Hull University Press, Hull.
5 K Leahy (1986). A dated stone axe-hammer from Cleethorpes, South Humberside. *Proceedings of the Prehistoric Society* 52, 143-52.

Other Bibliography

S Ellis, H Fenwick, M Lillie and R Van de Noort (ed.), (2001), *Wetland Heritage of the Lincolnshire Marsh: an archaeological survey.* Humber Wetlands Project Hull.
N Loughlin and K R Miller (1979), *A Survey of Archaeological Sites in Humberside.* Humberside Libraries and Amenities, Hull.
G Oliver (1825), *The Monumental Antiquities of Great Grimsby*, Isaac Wilson, Hull.

2. SOME NORTH LINCOLNSHIRE HISTORIANS

by Nick Lyons

HISTORIANS, BY VIRTUE OF PECULIARITIES in character and literary performance, can become quite as interesting as the histories they write. What they do, anyway, is strange, for it is scarcely normal to collect, interpret and publish information about the past – much of the material that interests historians having been deliberately concealed or discarded in the first place – whilst even the most humble of them has to assume superior attitudes in judging those who have gone before.

Local historians – who do not pursue their calling to make a living for the most part, and who may sometimes be fairly accused of mere nosiness, throw up amongst their number a weird variety of individuals who publicly display their personal obsessions and occasional grudges. It helps, in understanding these people, to remember that their published works have very rarely made, or promised to make, any profit at all. Indeed, often substantial losses were incurred by those same books that now command outrageous prices as 'collectors' items', and which, once purchased, are carefully shelved, polished, perhaps insured, but not usually read or understood. All helps to sustain the self-serving mystique of the provincial antiquarian seeking at least a good brick-built tower, ivory ones being in short supply in this field.[1]

The study of historians and their ideas, called historiography, has increasingly spread to local history.[2] For Lincolnshire, there is available *Some Historians of Lincolnshire*,[3] which considers in detail the work of a dozen or so writers of the nineteenth and twentieth centuries. But there were many more, various in their intentions, achievements and reputations. The work of those briefly considered in this chapter is intended to illustrate this variety.

Abraham de la Pryme
Best known to modern historians for his passing comments on the historical remains of his own day and the local memories that had been kept alive, is Abraham de la Pryme (1671-1704). His diary

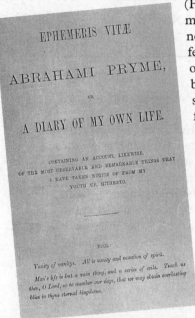

EPHEMERIS VITÆ

ABRAHAMI PRYME,

OR,

A DIARY OF MY OWN LIFE.

CONTAINING AN ACCOUNT, LIKEWISE,
OF THE MOST OBSERVABLE AND REMARKABLE THINGS THAT
I HAVE TAKEN NOTICE OF FROM MY
YOUTH UP, HITHERTO.

ECCL.·

Vanity of vanitys. All is vanity and vexation of spirit.
Man's life is but a vain thing, and a series of evils. Teach us
then, O Lord, so to number our days, that we may obtain everlasting
bliss in thyne eternal kingdome.

Figure 1. Abraham de la Pryme's own title page to his Diary, as set up in Charles Jackson's edited version of 1870. *Author's collection*

(Figure 1) is frequently cited as the source for morsels of enlightening information about north Lincolnshire at a time from which very few similar records survive. He was grandson of a Protestant refugee from Ypres who had been associated with the Axholme drainage schemes in the early seventeenth century. The family settled at Hatfield, near Doncaster, and the young Abraham appears to have been brought up entirely with English habits. Educated at home and at St John's College, Cambridge, he was ordained in 1693 and became curate of Broughton, near Brigg, in 1695, remaining only three years before returning to Hatfield. He went to Hull, as curate of the High Church, in 1698, and in 1701 was presented to the living of Thorne, but died of a fever in June, 1704.

During his short life, de la Pryme published only a handful of contributions to the transactions of the Society of Antiquaries, but he did collect much topographical information and had begun to compile a number of histories in manuscript. At Cambridge, his preference had been for natural history, chemistry (as it was then understood) and magic, but some of his historical investigation dated from that time. Once ordained, he turned increasingly to topographical matters and compiled materials for studies of Ripon, Selby, Doncaster, Hedon, York, Beverley, Hull, Winterton, and the levels of Hatfield Chase.

Abraham de la Pryme's reputation in respect of Lincolnshire rests on that part of his Diary relating to his years at Broughton. The Diary, his *Ephemeris Vitae*, was begun when he was twelve years of age with an account of his life to that time. He continued it, sometimes haphazardly, but always with wit and interest, for the rest of his life. The manuscript surviving, an edited version was issued in 1870 by the Surtees Society, which specialised in scholarly texts of Yorkshire interest – hence the full title: *The Diary of Abraham de la Pryme, the Yorkshire Antiquary.*[4]

Summary of such a book is impossible; only sampling can give some idea of the content. On his way to Cambridge in 1690, passing through Lincoln, he noted that 'several stately houses and churches are let fall to the ground', so that there was 'scarce anything worth seeing in it now but the high street'. Going for the first time into north Lincolnshire in 1695, he was struck by the great commons, like Egypt or Arabia 'which I had a most clear idea of when I beheld these sandy plains'. Caistor he found 'but a little place' despite its 'great markets and fairs', yet with 'a great many modern buildings' put up since the great fire there in 1681 or 1682.

At the same place, he saw his first Roman remains since coming into the county, and remarked on the many artificial hills along the road from Barton to Horncastle. He recorded, without comment, the claim that there were so many marine losses along the Lincolnshire coast that 'people are forc'd to leave their harvest and carry [the bodies] away in carts to bury them'. He discovered, with particular delight, that not only did his parish of Broughton sit on the great Roman Ermine Street, but that the original pavement could, in places, be discovered.

Although in a remote part of the country, he recorded people's reactions to major national events and, when William III included Lincoln on his Royal progress of 1695, noted the ceremonies, the crowds and the way prices suddenly increased. But, arguably, it is his comments on ancient ruined sites that matter most; he saw medieval lost villages where walls still stood, and remains of minor monastic houses known by the nineteenth century only from marks at, or below, ground level. Ruins of religious structures roused his High Protestant feelings: both the building works on the River Ancholme and the town of Grimsby, he believed, had fallen into decay because local people sacrilegiously robbed stone from monasteries to create mundane, non-spiritual structures.

Doing justice to the Diary is made more difficult because we do not know how de la Pryme would have matured as an historian. Long after his death, his *History of Winterton* was published,[5] but the original was obviously incomplete and unpolished, being neither coherent, nor much of it about Winterton. He left no disciples, no intellectual heirs in north Lincolnshire, no-one else to probe, observe and record. Throughout the eighteenth century, a handful of educated men – such as George Stovin of Winterton, through whom the manuscript history of that place was saved – collected documents, but largely ignored the remains of ancient structures.

After 1800, a new generation of clergymen adopted local history as their own, beginning to perceive it as one of their duties to secure knowledge of any obvious antiquities in their parishes, to inform ignorant parishioners, and perhaps to keep themselves mentally active in what was often a deadening environment.

George Oliver

A notable example of this can be found in the Reverend George Oliver (1782-1867). Born in Nottinghamshire, son of a schoolmaster who became an Anglican cleric, he in turn became assistant master or usher at Caistor Grammar School in 1803.[6] He stayed for six years, then moved to the mastership of King Edward's School, Grimsby. During the twelve years he held the post, he became ordained and was Vicar of Clee from 1815. In 1831, he took the vicarage of Scopwick – which he held for the rest of his life – although in 1834 he also took the parish of Wolverhampton. He then managed his parishes by employing various curates, but in 1847 exchanged Wolverhampton for South Hykeham, allowing his interests to be concentrated in Lincolnshire.

Oliver had no formal educational qualifications when he began as a schoolmaster, but, as was not uncommon then, was able to qualify for a degree from the University of Cambridge merely by keeping his name on college books for ten years. He then sought ordination. This is not to imply that he was no scholar, but his scholarship was idiosyncratic and probably would have been recognised had he taken the more orthodox course of attending university as an undergraduate.

His preoccupation was the study of Freemasonry, particularly its rites and ceremonies – a field in which imaginative speculation ran rife, whatever apparently scholarly proofs and references could be invoked.[7] His passage through the ranks of Freemasonry created much tension and, ultimately, scandal, but does not seem to have influenced his local studies – although it may be argued that the speculative nature of much Masonic history, was antithetical to the increasingly precise scholarship involved in collecting and understanding the concrete materials of topographical and social history.

Oliver's great outpourings on Masonic history were directed at Freemasons. Some were written to justify accusations made by non-masons, but the public in general did not matter to him in this respect: yet Oliver wrote a substantial body of local history which was clearly directed at a wider readership. The results were not always, perhaps not often, encouraging, and modern historians find him difficult to use or recommend. One commentator, otherwise sympathetic to Oliver, has remarked that he was 'a great antiquary and yet a small one', who was 'immense in facts, yet quite unable to do justice to them'.[8]

His first work of local history, *The Monumental Antiquities of Great Grimsby*, was published in 1825; there were to follow studies of Beverely, Sleaford, Wolverhampton, of monastic remains in

Lincolnshire, and 'existing remains of the ancient Britons'. Throughout the 1820s and 1830s, he contributed notes on Lincolnshire to the *Gentleman's Magazine*. Most of his local histories were formulaic. He began with reference to *Domesday Book* and noted any standing structures – preferably ruins – in order to establish the place's 'high antiquity'. Next, he dropped in the names of one or two would-be noble land-owning families from the Middle Ages, which led him to the church and a description of its features. Sometimes he concentrated upon the church alone. This approach was not his own invention, but one generally favoured at a time when few other models existed, libraries were not available to the public, and documentary sources lost or undiscovered.

Oliver refused to let such disadvantages limit his vision, which rose above the mundane. Thus his *Monumental Antiquities of Great Grimsby,* a rare book that commands high prices among collectors – is 'inaccurate and wildly imaginative';[9] his notes on Caistor contributed to the *Gentleman's Magazine* include a detailed and largely unjustified account of the Roman 'castle' there, complete with its 'subterranean passage, either for escape if hard pressed, or for the secret admission of troops or provisions'.

The larger part of Oliver's published work on local history appeared between 1825 and 1838, but the most curious came at the end of his life: *Ye Byrde of Gryme: an Apologue*[10] (Figure 2). As an account of Grimsby's development, it was written as dialogue between an unnamed narrator and a talking raven encountered in a dream. This raven was 'one of the mystical birds of Odin', symbolic of memory, and immortal. He came in AD645 with the Viking Gryme ('which was one of the forty-nine names of Odin'), and remained to protect Havelock and ensure Grimsby's foundation. The text continues for 280 pages, with digressions and descriptive passages, but surprisingly few attempts to draw the moral lessons concerning human nature from past events that we might expect in a work of the time.

Nominally, there are five sections – *The Mechanism* (Grimsby's origins,

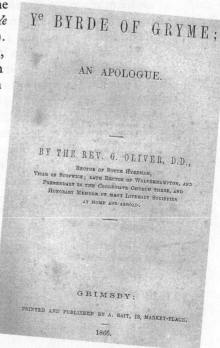

Figure 2. *Ye Byrde of Gryme,* as printed by A Gait, Grimsby, in 1866.
Author's collection

conceived to justify the story of Gryme); *Social Characteristics*; *Religious Antiquities*; *Municipals* and *Commerce* – but each is divided into chapters. Chronology is respected, giving the main structure, but does not dominate, and Oliver confidently refers his readers back and forth throughout the centuries to pursue a theme or make a point, in the belief that:

> ...*the increasing intelligence of the age... requires the adoption of some new and striking method of dressing up antiquarian truths in such a garb as may interest the feelings as well as inform the mind.*

Much of the book remains very engaging, as long as the reader has some background knowledge, but it is not a good introduction to the history of Grimsby and probably never was.

Ye Byrde of Gryme is dedicated to the inhabitants of Grimsby and Clee, amongst whom Oliver had not been resident since 1831. His career after that date had become confused because of his ill-considered acceptance of the living of Wolverhampton, and by complex Masonic disputes that had seen him dismissed as Deputy Provincial Master of Lincolnshire. In Grimsby, he had been secure and successful, so the work was 'a souvenir, and a kindly farewell' to a place he remembered with affection. Peculiar as the book is, it does no harm if seen as a curiosity in keeping with the tastes of its time, particularly the anxiety to understand the past in a spirit of romantic medievalism, mourning the loss of certain ancient grandeur yet emphasising that modern life was in every mundane way superior to the often miserable, disease-ridden existence of our ancestors.

Thus, in ancient Grimsby, we are assured every merchant's dwelling was 'indeed spacious and stately', town festivities were heralded 'with ringing bells and other solemnities', everything was 'quaint' and modern times began in the seventeenth century. However, modern Grimsby had proper local government and drains, and so was really better than the town in former centuries. The device of the talking raven would not have been strange to readers brought up on the fantasies of Barham's *Ingoldsby Legends* (1840, 1847), the work of Edgar Allan Poe, Kingsley's *Water Babies* (1863), and who, in the same year as *Ye Byrde* was published, would be faced by the oddities of *Alice in Wonderland*.[11]

Poulson, Ball and others

In the year when Oliver brought out his first major work, *The History and Antiquities of the Town and Minster of Beverley* (Beverley, 1829) there had appeared George Poulson's *Beverlac, or The Antiquities and*

History of the Town of Beverley (London). Poulson (1782-1858) was to make his name as the historian of the East Riding of Yorkshire, going on to produce the monumental *History and Antiquities of the Seigniory of Holderness* (two volumes, Hull, 1840-41) based on materials gathered by William Dade, rector of Barmston. His background and life are problematical. Apparently from a well-to-do family in the metal trades in Hampshire and Gloucestershire, very little is known of him until he entered Magdalen College, Oxford, as a gentleman commoner in 1823, aged thirty-eight. Effectively, this meant that he enjoyed all the privileges money could buy without having to prove himself academically. Gentlemen commoners were usually titled or otherwise well connected. He took no degree, and mysteriously reappears as author of *Beverlac* a few years later.

For reasons now lost, Poulson left Yorkshire and settled in Barrow-upon-Humber, perhaps as early as 1833, where he remained. It looks as if he sought some kind of haven there. Directories sometimes describe him as 'postmaster', sometimes as 'gentleman'. Census enumerations returns reveal him in 1841 as head of a household consisting otherwise of John Metcalfe, an agricultural labourer, and Metcalfe's aged wife and daughter. Ten years later he was at a different address, with only Metcalfe's daughter as his housekeeper. He was unmarried both times, described as 'independent'. A recent commentator has noted that 'from the odd remark about women found in his writings he seems to have been very much a confirmed bachelor'.[12]

Poulson became acquainted with Henry William Ball of Barton-on-Humber, who came from a family of printers. William's grandfather, Thomas Ball, was working in Brigg in the first decade of the nineteenth century, and Charles Ball, father of Henry, was established in Barton by 1842, at the Imperial Press Office, Market Lane. Mary Ball, presumably Charles' widow, published *The Lindsey Observer* (*c.*1854 to 1857) and was succeeded by Henry William who issued *The Barton, Brigg, Caistor & Winterton News* (1858 to 1863). He continued in business until his death in 1914, combining printing, aspects of stationery work, and book dealing. He was widely known as a specialist in antiquarian books, and parts of his personal collections survive today as museum material.

Local histories were proliferating across England in the 1850s; many were expensively produced, massive volumes containing materials collected by self-indulgent gentleman scholars over a lifetime, and financed by subscription. They were not intended for the general market. At the same time, the new railways were encouraging production of shorter works for sale to the tourists who, if they were not yet the cut-price crowds which later thronged the seaside resorts, would never-the-less baulk at paying more than a shilling or so for a pamphlet.

North Lincolnshire in 1850 was served by very few local historians; on the shelves of the well-to-do might be the histories of Axeholme by Peck (1815) and Stonehouse (1839), perhaps along with Oliver's *Grimsby*. There might also be Allen and Saunders' *History of the County of Lincoln* (two volumes, 1834) and Saunders' *Lincolnshire in 1836*, the latter important for its 'nearly one hundred engravings' – although the north of the county was somewhat sparsely covered. In more ordinary households there might be William Andrew's humbler history of Winterton and district (1836), and perhaps Greenwood's *Picturesque Tour to Thornton Monastery* (Hull, 1835) – but even this cost three shillings and sixpence (17^1/$_2$p) new.[13] It is worth recalling that the full title of successful commercial directories often ran: *History, Gazetteer, and Directory*, and that entries for individual places in such volumes carried a brief account of such antiquities as were known.[14]

Henry William Ball is remembered today for the little book familiarly called *Ball's Barton* (Figures 3 & 4), actually *The Social*

Figure 3. An engraving of St Peter's Church which appears in Henry William Ball's history of Barton-upon-Humber. *Author's collection*

History and Antiquities of Barton-upon-Humber, printed by Mary Ball in 1856. It is an unassuming volume with a handful of modest engravings, yet was an important contribution to local studies in north Lincolnshire, and although very much the product of its time, remains a significant reference point. Ball's commercial sense was probably as strong a motivation as any scholarly ambitions that he may have harboured, although he never saw a reprint of the work. The authorship is a matter of confusion, however. Ball was not himself even the publisher – that was his mother. Nor did he write most of it; there is a brief, un-headed note at the beginning, over Ball's name, explaining that the 'first part' (in fact, seventy-two pages out of ninety-six) is based on the collection and unpublished works of the late W S Hesleden, edited by George Poulson. The 'second part' was apparently Ball's work, and he acknowledges the help of the Reverend J Byron[15] and 'other gentlemen'. He describes himself as 'the compiler'.[16]

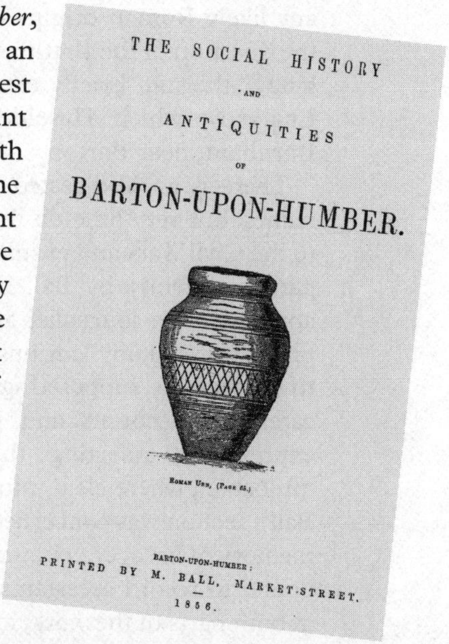

Figure 4. Cover page of Henry William Ball's history of Barton-upon-Humber, printed by Mary Ball in 1856. *Author's collection*

Hesleden, Poulson and Byron are sufficiently interesting in their own right to merit separate investigation.[17] Poulson seems to have sought obscurity, and was apparently not even the subject of any sort of memoir in East Yorkshire until recently, although there is an entry – albeit brief and inaccurate – for him in the *Dictionary of National Biography,* and his brief obituary notice in *The Gentleman's Magazine* pronounced his book on Holderness 'one of the best topographical works of modern times'.

Hesleden is forgotten because he published little, and his collections relating to the history of Barton, Barrow and Thornton Abbey are lost, or mislaid, at least to public view. Byron again published little, but appeal was repeatedly made to him in his own time as an authority on local history.

An orthodox approach is the marked characteristic of the *Social History*, although Poulson offered a sensitive warning against conjectural accounts of very early settlement where, as in Barton's case, there were no documentary sources; so he refused to discuss any likely Roman origins of the town. He showed similar care over the question of the Battle of Brunnenburgh (AD937, when the Saxon king, Athelstan briefly established the dominance of Wessex across England), which Heselden had sought to prove was fought at Burnham, near Barton.

There is an ill-digested medieval section, notes on families, place names, but very little on the Reformation period, and slight reference to the Civil Wars and ensuing republic as 'the Usurpation'. The second part, apparently by Ball himself, is different in tone, revealing the approach of a journalist anxious to assert the quaintness of former times, to retell any 'curious and romantic' legend, and by implication to censure the supposed ignorance of the past. Whereas Poulson was careful in accounts and judgements, Ball was content to slip in expressions asserting that such-and-such an occurrence was 'probable', where clear information was lacking. Fortunately, much of Ball's section was concerned with recent times and events within living memory of his age, a circumstance in which even journalists are largely bound to record ascertainable materials. There is much that is useful in both parts of the work, important in differing ways and degrees, and often for the assumption made by the writers that show the contemporary mind-set; yet the book is not very easy to read. There is no continuous thread, no theme, and little analysis. Typical of its time, it must be used with care, and cannot be treated as a last resort or a definitive statement of what Barton was like in past times.

Local historians, and their readers, perceive various uses and values in their subject at different times and as the circumstances of society alter. The search for 'ultimate history' at higher levels of national and international development is associated with certain nineteenth century writers who broadly believed that it was possible to assemble all the facts, thus enabling an absolute understanding of any given situation in the past to emerge of its own accord. This reduced the need for interpretation and the possibility of argument among historians, themselves. Local historians pursued a superficially similar, but less refined, course. They needed to find something to say about their chosen area for each historical period, and might be tempted to extrapolate generously from slight evidence to fill the gaps.

Ball's compilation, and most of Oliver's work, can be accounted to be of this sort – which makes the more worthy Poulson's refusal to speculate about the Roman origins of Barton, and his inclusion of Hesleden's ideas about Brunnenburgh, only so 'that the reader may form his own opinion'.[18]

The Social History and Antiquities of Barton is self-evidently an attempt to bring together all the information available, allowing Ball to invoke in his press advertisements the names of three well-respected local antiquarians, and boast that 'nearly One Hundred Pounds' had been spent 'in obtaining copies of documents, and information'.[19] But Ball was, by experience and inclination, a commercial animal. Oliver's motivation had developed from what seems to have been merely a love of didacticism (related, perhaps, to a desire to please his clerical superiors through a fashionable devotion to the ancient roots of the Church of England), to a recognition that over-much attention to the 'details of local topography' could 'appear uninviting even to those who feels a certain degree of interest' in the subject. This might hinder people's recognition of 'the gradual improvements which have been introduced by the inevitable progress of arts, sciences, and human invention'.[20] Oliver came to a pragmatic vision of the study of history – it allowed mankind to perceive better the simple advantages of living in nineteenth century England.

Comparison of Oliver and Ball (or perhaps Ball's circus) with de la Pryme is irrelevant. De la Pryme's *Diary* was never intended for publication, is not a history of anything except himself, and, as edited, is an historical document in its own right. Had Oliver and Ball had access to the manuscript, they would have extracted relevant entries for their own works. In fact, both are noticed by the editors of the *Diary* for their own histories, as Poulson, to amplify de la Pryme's notes. De la Pryme's purpose in writing was wholly different to theirs – he set out to record 'the most observable and remarkable things' of his times. This avoidance of the mundane means that we learn nothing of his daily routine; only the unusual is recorded, but often in such an allusive way that, without the editor's notes and commentary, we could not appreciate many passages. The Diary thus remains a personal record, putting the modern reader into the privileged position of the spy or *voyeur*.

This helps to explain why, although in the edited form it is a work of heavy scholarship, it is much more fun to read than the dry listings of Ball's compilation and the mannered prose of George Oliver's *jeu d'esprit*.

Notes and References

1   Edward Peacock, the great nineteenth century antiquarian and dialect collector of Bottesford and Kirton in Lindsey, built himself a pseudo-Gothic brick tower to his library at Bottesford Manor – see E Elder, *The Peacock Lincolnshire Word Books* (Scunthorpe Museum Society, 1997), and her various articles in the journal of the Society for Lincolnshire History and Archaeology.
2   For example, C R J Currie & C P Lewis, *A Guide to English County Histories* (Stroud, 1994).

3   C Sturman, editor, *Some Historians of Lincolnshire* (Society for Lincolnshire History and Archaeology, 1992).

4   Surtees Society, Volume LIV, for the year MDCCCLXIX. The nominal editor was Charles de la Pryme, head of the family and owner of the original manuscript, but the notes and transcriptions are the work of others. Most of the Lincolnshire element was the work of Edward Peacock.

5   *History of Winterton, in the County of Lincoln*, by Abraham de la Pryme; with an Introduction by Edward Peacock, Esq., FSA, the owner of the original manuscript, *Archaeologia*, Volume XL (1866).

6   R S E Sandbach, *Priest and Freemason* (1988), p.22 & c.; and Dixon & Coxon, *Caistor Grammar School Records* (Caistor, 1933), 41.

7   See Sandbach, *passim*, in which, however, the complex and arcane practices of the *Craft* overwhelm any attempt to understand Oliver as an individual or a scholar.

8   Ibid., 172.

9   E Gillett, *A History of Grimsby*, 184.

10 Grimsby, A Gait, 1866.

11 Oliver may have been influenced by an anonymous attempt to raise interest in the history of Boston, *Boston in the Olden Times: a Series of Legends and tales* (Boston, Noble, 1840). In this publication, the ghost of a Franciscan friar, encountered in Boston Stump, recounts the story. The volume was intended as the first in a series, *Traditions of Lincolnshire*, but no more appear to have been published.

12 See M T Craven, *A New and Complete History of the Borough of Hedon* (Driffield, 1972).

13 In 1843 in Lincolnshire, one shilling a day was considered a fair wage for women's day-labour on the land – cp report of Mr Denison in *Reports of Special Assistant Poor Law Commissioners on the Employment of Women and Children in Agriculture* (HMSO, 1843).

14 E.g. White 1842, 1856.

15 The Reverend John Byron (Vicar of North Killingholme, 1842-1886). His family owned the (now effectively lost) Tudor mansion house and land in Killingholme. John's grandfather (died 1844) was Vicar of Keelby for fifty-two years and, briefly, of Killingholme as well. John took the same parishes. He was active in many fields, and well known as an antiquary. He wrote a *Handbook for Visitors to Thornton Abbey* (London & Hull, 1851), and was an early member of the Lincoln Diocesan Architectural Society, guiding the Society's visit to Barrow Castles in May, 1859.

16 Part I, 3.

17 William Smith Hesleden (1777-1852) was eldest son of William Hesleden, solicitor of Barton-upon-Humber who, like his father, followed scholarly pursuits in his leisure time. He lived in Barrow-on-Humber, where his brother, the Reverend Edward Hesleden, was vicar from 1805 to 1828. He followed his father's profession, and his practice was extensive. His obituary notice in *The Gentleman's Magazine* noted that he enjoyed 'an enviable but deserved reputation'. Surprisingly little is known of his local collections, although notes, contributions to the press, and copies of maps turn up from time to time, bearing his unmistakable initials. Ball acquired some of his collections, passing them, perhaps temporarily, to Poulson; others were known to Edward Peacock, A R Maddison and Peter Binnall. Few are in public collections. In his lifetime, he was generous with his knowledge; Robert Franklin, the Barrow poet, thanked him for historical information in the Preface to his collection *The House of Brocklesby* (Hull, 1852), and it is likely he was responsible for the text of Greenwood's *Picturesque Tour to Thornton Monastery*. For a brief account of Hesleden, see F Henthorn, *The History of Brigg Grammar School* (1959).

18 Part I, 3.

19 R C Russell et al, *Barton on Humber in the 1850s: Part I* (Barton WEA, 1973); non-paginated, but see p.13.

20 *Ye Byrde of Gryme*, p.1. His investigations of Masonic history were in the eyes of fellow masons intended more simply 'to disseminate a knowledge of the principles and benefits of Masonry' – memoir of Oliver, in *The Origin of the Royal Arch Order of Masonry* (new edition, 1867), xxix.

Acknowledgements

With thanks for the help given by library staff at Scunthorpe, Barton-upon-Humber, Hull and, particularly, Beverley.

3. WALKING THE CLAY BANK

by Richard S Clarke

ALTHOUGH, HISTORICALLY, THE HUMBER ESTUARY has been a barrier – separating the Anglo Saxon kingdoms of Northumbria and Mercia as well as the counties of East Yorkshire and Lindsey – it has also been a highway for ferries and sea-borne freight, connecting its north and south banks on an everyday basis. From all points along the estuary the opposite bank is visible, more so as it narrows inland and the rising ground levels draw the traveller's attention to the environment of the opposite bank as well as to his immediate surroundings.

The south bank of the Humber Estuary is very accessible to walkers and cyclists by means of the man-made clay, or reinforced, bank that contains its twenty feet tidal range waters. The Humber is Eastern England's most expansive estuary, one fifth of the nation's land drains into it and the vast, ecologically valuable mudflats revealed up-estuary of Hull at low tide, along with the warpland sections of either bank, are the products of millennia of post-glacial silt deposition. The estuary, the landward terrain and agricultural land use, associated industries past and present, historic settlements and transport networks, panoramic views and internationally important sites for nature conservation, all blend to define a region of undervalued fascination.

There are tentative plans to define a new, long distance footpath from Cleethorpes, at the mouth of the Humber, to the mouth of the River Trent at its head. For most of its length, the south bank of the Humber is defined by a man-made structure commonly known as the 'clay bank' which, in its various forms, prevents inundation of the inland warplands and, for much of its route, supports a public right of way. It also forms the northern boundary of the unitary authorities of North and North East Lincolnshire.

The coastline between North Coates and Cleethorpes is a zone of transition between the North Sea coast of Lincolnshire and the Humber mouth; here, the claybank divides saltmarsh from agricultural warplands that are still known as the Marsh, and the dip slope of the Lincolnshire Wolds can be seen rising in the middle distance. The Humber Mouth Yacht Club house and Humberstone

Fitties provide a convenient starting point for walkers – the latter being a rare, surviving and complete 1920s and 1930s 'hutment colony', with some cabins boasting many original features. The history of this site has been recorded by the Humberstone Fitties Preservation Society (contact Cleethorpes Tourist Information Centre) and, in recent years, one of these cabins has been open to the public on the national Heritage Weekend in mid-September.

A cluster of Scots pine at the northern end of the Fitties forms a prominent landmark on this expansive lowland coast. Between here and the 1960s Leisure Centre that forms a bastion at the end of Cleethorpes 'prom', is one mile of sand dunes secured by tough leafed grasses and shrubs and backed by an asphalt topped clay bank. Seaward, a complex area of encroaching saltmarsh, pools and channels give way at low tide to vast, sandy expanses. Natural access points intersect the dunes and offer up natural, uninhabited haunts. The car park, accessed from near the boating lake, and M T Bellys (that name is genuine) Mobile café provide a valuable service to devotees of this area.

A standard concrete promenade from the Leisure Centre, reaching to well beyond the Pier, defines the hustle and bustle of a seaside town environment. Many bye-law housing streets strike off at right angles, while well preserved Victorian wrought-iron shop fronts grace the pierhead area. Seaview Street, and the mini roundabout at its junction with the promenade's top road, was where the resort first developed seaward from the early village of Old Clee with its part-Norman church. Cleethorpes' 'end of the line' railway station stands beside the 'prom', ensuring the train is still a favoured option for many day-trippers.

From all points so far defined, ships of various types are almost always visible out in the Humber mouth, with Spurn Point, the southern tip of the Yorkshire coast, beyond and the two Great War anti-submarine forts standing as bleak reminders of those fearful times.

Today, the built up areas of Cleethorpes and Grimsby merge; the walker must leave the seafront as the Grimsby docks complex accepts no public right of way. Larry Malkin, in his book *Wavelength Wanderings along the Humber Estuary* (1992), defines an interesting suggested route through Grimsby and back out to the estuary clay bank beyond.

To return to the Humber bank north west of Grimsby Docks, the walker/cyclist must follow the grass verge of the A180, past acres of imported cars awaiting distribution, on to Morton Lane at the roundabout, and so to a right of way beside a reedy inlet. From here

Figure 1. *Pyewipe, with a view up the Humber Estuary. Author's collection*

to East Halton Skitter is approximately ten miles of continuous concrete bank (leaving out the extent of Immingham Dock), forming a promenade ideal for all weather access. Immediately one reaches the concrete bank, expansive panoramic views unfold (in clear weather) up and down the estuary, dominated to the east by the Tuscan-like Grimsby Dock Tower and the Victorian dock offices. To the north, one can see the undulating landscape of Holderness and, to the north-west, the deep-water jetties of Immingham Dock with Saltend, Hull Docks and city, backed by the distant Yorkshire Wolds. Known as Pyewipe (Figure 1), this area is part of the flat coastal lowlands that stretch five miles inland to the dip slope of the Lincolnshire Wolds – in effect the northern end of the Lincolnshire Marsh. Initially, it may seem uninteresting, dominated as it is by a series of industrial complexes inland of the concrete bank, but it should really be assessed in the context of the whole panorama. Historically, church steeples were significant aids to navigation and Patrington and Ottringham church spires across in Holderness remain prominent features in this panorama, visible at all points from Cleethorpes to Goxhill Marsh.

The huge significance of the Humber Estuary for nature conservation is immediately made clear at Pyewipe. A birdwatching hide stands beside the inlet, while nearby is an interpretative board explaining the Estuary's international importance as an overwintering area for migrant birds and all season waders; it also defines the intertidal mudflats as the Estuary's 'larder'. This is an area where one may pause to reflect how tightened regulations governing industrial effluent discharge is so well exemplified by modern attempts to reconcile industry and environment.

Setting off north-west, one encounters linear colonies of saltmarsh at the head of the inter-tidal zone, formed where salt tolerant plants colonise the silt. Here, as well as on the especially large areas on the upper estuary, is formed one of Europe's most important regions of saltmarsh habitat. On reaching a linear plantation east of Immingham Dock, the right of way diverts inland and the traveller has to follow the road system into and through Immingham. Again, the grass verge of a dual carriageway has to be followed to a roundabout, this time at South Killingholme oil refinery, where the right and then left turns bring one to Marsh Lane and on through an industrial site to the concrete bank. This long detour is unfortunate and made hazardous in places by a shortfall of pavement provision. However, many fields beside Marsh Lane remain as permanent pasture, in contrast to the predominantly arable cultivation on the coastal plain, serving to remind us that the initial reason for parliamentary enclosure in this area was to define 'ings land' summer grazing; the pastureland in turn enhances biodiversity.

Here at Killingholme Marshes, the coastal plain has narrowed to three miles width, although the dip slope beyond East Halton Beck rises very gradually. Immediately inland of the concrete bank are a series of large arable fields set by a post-enclosure field pattern. Over the fields and beyond Burkinshaw's Covert plantation, huge oil storage tanks covering hundreds of acres are visible. Soon after rejoining the concrete bank, one encounters a fascinating, almost incongruous, collection of three old lighthouses (Figure 2). Arthur Storey, in his book *Hull Trinity House History of Pilotage and Navigational Aids of the River Humber (1512–1908)*, recounts their construction in 1836 and 1851 '...as a transit course from Spurn'. The tallest of the three was rebuilt in 1875 following damage by lightning. It still carries a flashing beacon, as does its near neighbour. The third, with its adjoining lighthouse keeper's cottage, is in private

Figure 2. Killingholme lighthouses and concrete 'prom'. *Author's collection*

ownership.

Nearing North Killingholme Haven, a large network of lakes with managed peripheral reedbeds, is home to a large population of wetland birds. This is the first of many such areas between here and South Ferriby identifying locations where clay was dug for brick and pantile-making factories between the early nineteenth and mid-twentieth centuries. These post-industrial sites greatly enhance biodiversity, many being owned by the Lincolnshire Trust (for Nature Conservation). Immediately west of the Haven is a large, private port complex with a deep water jetty for container ships that supports its neighbouring nature reserve by providing roosting and feeding opportunities. Inland, there are two gas-fired electric power stations, representing the 'dash for gas' of the 1990s in order to reduce CO_2 emissions. Thankfully, there is a public right of way through the site.

The final section of concrete 'prom' passes another claypit, here with the disused kilns and chimney still standing. The open land of East Halton 'marsh' inland and the wide estuary seaward make this a bracing stretch, and from this point, the Humber Bridge becomes visible, apparently inland, but in fact around the dogleg bend of the estuary. Across the estuary, the towers of Paull and Hedon churches still form significant landmarks, although the city and docks of Hull and the power station and chemical plant at Saltend tend to demand more attention.

Up estuary of North Killingholme Haven, the South Humber bank becomes almost entirely rural in character. The mouth of East Halton Skitter is ecologically and historically fascinating, best seen at low tide when plunging mudbanks are separated by a narrow, gushing channel. It was this modest stream, draining the spring line villages along the base of the Lincolnshire Wolds, that linked three pre-Reformation monastic sites. Cottam nunnery was the furthest inland, near present-day Keelby; downstream, the first Premonstratensian priory stood, also near present-day Keelby; finally, three miles upstream from the estuary, there was a huge Augustinian abbey at Thornton whose magnificent brick gatehouse is still standing. To these medieval monastic personnel, rivers and estuary were highways, and there is even documentary evidence of trade with the Cistercian abbey at Meaux in Holderness.

Between the mouth of the Skitter and Goxhill Haven (also known as Goxhill Ferry) the clay bank is separated from the estuary waters by a wide expanse of saltmarsh and mudflats at low tide. Inland, mature hawthorn hedges divide rectangular post-Enclosure fields, while across the estuary Hull, Hull Docks and Paull, with its now residential lighthouse contemporary with those at Killingholme, appear to be almost within reach. From here to North Ferriby, the contrast between north and south banks is reversed.

Coming to the evocatively named 'Dawson City' (Figure 3) on the

Figure 3. Remains of a disused trawler at the breaker's yard between Goxhill Haven and New Holland. *Author's collection*

dogleg bend of the Humber, one finds another post-industrial wetland nature reserve. Looking back, views of Killingholme Haven, Immingham and Grimsby are now left behind, while ahead, views up-estuary to and beyond the Humber Bridge provide a completely new panorama.

The three-mile section of claybank between Goxhill Haven and New Holland fronts a wide expanse of open farmland. There are no hedges to provide variety, so inevitably one's attention is drawn to the varied urban landscape across the estuary, spanning the floodplain of the River Hull.

New Holland jetty remains the most prominent man-made structure, apart from the Humber Bridge, on this section of the estuary. Built in the 1840s by the Manchester, Sheffield and Lincolnshire Railway Company to access cross-Humber ferries, these extensive port facilities are in private ownership and provide a berth for merchant ships. When the Humber Bridge opened in 1981, the traditional paddle-driven ferries ceased business. They are now incongruously berthed for recreation purposes in Hartlepool Marina, Grimsby town dock and the Pool of London. Fortunately, a public right of way has been maintained through the dock complex and a short detour over a level crossing brings the walker to the original station hotel and an area of railway company housing called Manchester Square.

Immediately west of New Holland is the first of an almost continuous succession of claypits that once provided the raw material for brick and pantile making factories. There were over thirty of them between here and South Ferriby by the late nineteenth century. Most had wooden jetties so that Humber keels and barges could transport the finished products. Then the estuary would have thronged with boats, ships and ferries plying their business on this estuarine highway. Even today, at high tide, convoys of smaller merchant ships (compared with the ocean-going ships seen at Immingham and King George Dock, Hull) can be seen sailing up to Goole on the River Ouse, or at Gainsborough on the River Trent. From Hull 'upwards' the contrast between the estuary at high and low tide is remarkable. Vast expanses of mudflat are revealed at low water, providing valuable feeding grounds for waders. Salt water fish, such as halibut, can be caught on rod and line as far inland as the Humber Bridge at high tide, although the ability of the upper estuary to sustain fish life is naturally compromised by the heavy concentration of silt carried in suspension by the Trent and Ouse rivers.

At Barrow Haven, the public right of way passes through a small private wharf and over the railway bridge before returning to the clay bank. Once a medieval outport for the town of Barrow-upon-Humber, Barrow Haven is now a linear settlement straddling the Haven clay bank. Here, there was a Norman motte and bailey castle – evidenced by earthen ramparts indicating where the fringes of the estuary once were. The succession of clay pits to, and beyond, Barton-upon-Humber are fascinating, with nature reserves adjoining water-skiing and yachting lakes.

Barton is steeped in history, having developed from late Saxon times as the principal Humber port until Kingston-upon-Hull developed in the 1300s. It controlled the principal ferry crossing until the building of New Holland jetty. Developed in the shelter of dry valleys just above the estuary marsh, some of the modern 'suburban' housing commands fine panoramic views. East of the mouth of Barton Haven, a new country park is being created on land previously belonging to an estuary-side industrial complex.

A package of funding was secured by the joint efforts of local and national government to pay for clearing the site, for the removal of contaminated topsoil (to be replaced by warpland topsoil excavated west of the town) and for the planting, landscaping and building required. The project should be completed by 2003 and will greatly enhance the recreational and environmental facilities of the region. Already three wetland nature reserves and a new network of footpaths are completed, and soon a footbridge will span the lower Haven. Only a short distance inland from the footbridge is the Ropery craft centre incorporating a display on the history of the clay pits.

Crossing under the Humber Bridge carriageway and on past *Reeds Hotel* (an uneasy alliance between facilities benefiting from a natural environment and the welfare of that environment), the route passes the site of derelict, early 1900s cement works. Access to the foreshore exists and opens up superb views back to the Humber Bridge and Hull beyond. A little further on, at Chowder Ness, a jettied beacon denotes the deep-water channel that brings shipping very close to the south bank at this point in the estuary.

Beyond Barton Cliff, the slopes of the Wolds reach down to the foreshore – for it was here that the inter-glacial overflow channel broke through the chalk escarpment. A number of disused chalk quarries and the remnants of wooden, foreshore jetties testify to former industrial activity. The shingle foreshore of the boulder clay and chalk South Ferriby Cliff may be walked at low tide, but at other times a farm track above the Cliff must be taken, affording magnificent views up, and over, the upper estuary.

The traditional village of South Ferriby straddles the base of the scarp slope, but following the clay bank past the early 1800s brick Hall then takes one to the later linear development near the lock at the mouth of the River Ancholme. Here navigation between estuary and canalised river is controlled and, although overshadowed by the neighbouring cement works, a local marina adds colour and interest.

Unfortunately, at present, the Humber Bank along the remainder of the Vale of Ancholme, almost as far as Winteringham Haven, is not a public right of way. This includes the point north-east of Winteringham Grange where Roman Ermine Street reached the Abus (as it was named then) and accessed a crossing to Petuaria (present day Brough). The three-mile section of clay bank from Winteringham Haven to Whitton village defines Winteringham Marsh, a large area of warpland farmland leading to the northern end of the Lincolnshire Edge (limestone escarpment). Principal interest value is thus found in studying the saltmarsh and mudflats, and in the views across to the limestone hills above South Cave and the lowland of Wallingfen and the distant Vale of York.

Having walked through a short stretch of Whitton village, the public right of way is again accessed opposite the Norman church tower. In the hillside, here, the thin strata of the upper Lias escarpment can be seen. The route passes along the modest scarp slope known as the Devil's Causeway and so to the clay bank, with views over the deep water Whitton Channel, Whitton Sand nature reserve and the lock at the mouth of the Market Weighton Canal. The 440 hectares of agricultural warpland between here and the base of the prominent limestone escarpment at Alkborough has been designated by the Environment Agency as a 'setback' area, whereby the land will be allowed to flood in order to alleviate potential flood damage elsewhere. Thus a big, new wildlife habitat will be created to enhance the internationally important conservation status of the Humber and to link with other estuary bank regeneration initiatives in North Lincolnshire.

The beacon separating the mouths of the rivers Trent and Ouse marks the end of our south Humber side trek. Whether or not the current right of way from Trent Falls to Alkborough village will be maintained in the future remains to be seen; if not a return to Whitton will be necessary.

The south Humber bank route as outlined in this chapter is approximately thirty-eight miles in length, a similar distance, for example, to the Suffolk coast long distance path. There are potential problems: clear weather is vital to appreciate panoramic views, long distance clay bank walking can seem monotonous and the three sections where currently the walker has to divert inland are unfortunate. Many will, I hope, wish to walk sections of length and location suitable to themselves; those wishing to walk the complete distance will need three to four days, unless very resolute. Grimsby, Immingham, Barton and *Reed's Hotel* provide accommodation facilities.

While wondering how best to conclude this chapter, I drove to the small banktop carpark at Fairfield Pit immediately west of New Holland wharf. It was dark and cold, but the air was clear and I instinctively set to identifying points in the illuminated shorelines of Hull and Hessle. The Humber Bridge lights were clearly visible, while the jetty invited recollections of trains and ferries. The steel skeleton of a long abandoned barge loomed from the foreshore mud, while nearby a wader sounded a shrill but plaintive warning cry. Behind me, the many and varied occupants of the claypit roosted in peace. The lights of a distant ship moved silently out on the water of the estuary. Here, then, was a microcosm of the south Humber bank experience.

Notes and References

The Landranger Series OS maps (scale 1: 50000) are readily available and provide ample information to enhance the walker's experience. Sheet 113 covers the Humber mouth area and, inland to Goxhill Haven, Sheet 107 continues to Barton Cliff whilst Sheet 106 details the upper Humber.

4. THE FOUNDING LEGEND OF GRIMSBY

by Kevin Gracie

A FAMOUS ANCIENT BRITISH LEGEND tells us that Grimsby town was founded by a Danish settler named Grim. Many are sceptical of this claim, holding the opinion the story is purely myth or an old wives' tale. Yet one can forgive them, for even some learned scholars, too, have decided it is merely romanticism. Fortunately, however, there are some historians who have taken the matter very seriously. This differing of opinions illustrates only too well just why this particular legend is so famous and probably the most controversial.

According to the story, there had been an invasion into Denmark. It resulted in the death of the Danish king and a threat to the life of his son, Havelok the infant prince, from the usurper to the throne. Grim managed to rescue the child, provision a ship and, with Havelok and his family safely aboard, the fugitives fled – sailing to freedom across the sea to England. They survived an attack made by marauders and a storm in the North Sea, finding a safe haven and tidal creek off the Humber.

Landing at the site in his storm-battered ship and finding the area unoccupied, Grim decided to make it their new home. Buildings were made from the timbers of the ship, and Grim took up the life of a fisher, prospering greatly by supplying fish to all the marsh folk, to the city of Lincoln and to all the towns and villages in Lindsey. He raised Havelok as his own son.

Over the intervening years, other people were drawn to the place and the settlement grew. So, too, did Havelok. He reached manhood, tall and strong – a gentle giant, courteous, kind and true, and loved by all, helping to distribute and sell the fish and, by virtue of his strength, able to carry incredibly heavy basket loads that were impossible for ordinary men to lift. He forgot his former life and real identity – which was probably a blessing because, it was said, as a seven-year-old, he had seen his two little sisters murdered in cold blood and had witnessed the death of his mother. Grim kept silent about the truth, making plans and provisions having seen from the portents that one day Havelok would learn all and regain his rightful crown.

Then came a terrible time of drought and famine. Havelock sought service at the court of the king of Lindsey, at Lincoln. He found work as a porter and scullion in the royal kitchens and soon became a wonder in Lincoln because of his amazing strength and good nature. At a stone-throwing contest, Havelok managed to lift the great stone higher and hurl it a great deal further than anyone else.

The king of Lincoln, Alsi, had a ward – his niece, the fair princess Goldburga, whose southern kingdom he had held, in addition to his own, since she was a child. King Alsi had promised to give Goldburga's hand in marriage to the strongest and goodliest man in the land. Hearing of Havelok's wondrous reputation, he decided to marry her off to this kitchen knave, thereby shaming her and maintaining overall control of her kingdom. Yet the princess was comforted by a vision she had received in a dream, which had been interpreted for her by a hermit: Havelok would become a king and she, a queen. The hermit also advised them to return to Grimsby.

When they reached Grimsby, they discovered that Grim was dead. Not only did Grim's family reveal the truth about Havelok's identity but also the fact that he had amassed and hidden a large amount of wealth until the time it should be needed. Although gold and silver would not be enough to help Havelok regain the Danish throne, it did enable him to set sail for Denmark, along with the princess and his foster brothers and sisters. He was told to seek a loyal lord who had been waiting and preparing for his return.

Upon reaching Denmark, with the aid of a large army, Havelok regained his crown. Later, he returned to Lindsey with Goldburga and thousands of Danes. They successfully reclaimed Goldburga's kingdom from King Alsi as well as taking control of Lincoln. Just and peace loving, beloved by the people, they became united sovereigns over their three kingdoms in Denmark and England.

The legend and the borough seal

The seal of Great Grimsby (Figure 1) was fashioned sometime in the thirteenth century, possibly soon after King John granted the town its first charter in 1201 (although the town had been referred to as a borough long before that time). The seal is, without doubt, a rarity – being the only founding legendary municipal seal in the whole of Great Britain. It features the main characters of the local legend, with Grim centred prominently in a stance of readiness, holding his shield and drawn sword. Above him is a portrayal of the Hand of Providence, thought to have guided his actions; beneath him lies his helm, symbolising the fact he was the founder of the town. On either

Figure 1. Thirteenth century Grimsby Seal, depicting Grim, the legendary founder of the town, with Havelok and Goldburga. *www.stonefree.org*

side of Grim are representations of Havelok and Goldburga, with their crowns suspended above them indicating their royal status. Havelok is offering a ring to the princess betokening the fact they were eventually wed. The seal may clearly be a piece of material evidence that the early inhabitants of the borough believed the Grim legend was founded on fact.

From the time of the Norman Conquest until that of Elizabeth I, the legend of Grim and Havelok was one of England's most popular. Indeed, between the eleventh and thirteenth centuries, it seems to have been regarded as a classic. As claimed, the story may have authentic root origins in the sixth century prior to the Viking invasions, probably surviving by courtesy of bards, minstrels and other time honoured oral traditions. Yet, although the story has survived and still retains much of its original charm and fascination, it undoubtedly has suffered changes over the years.

The earliest surviving written record comes in the form of a Norman-French poem: the *Lai d'Haveloc*, believed to have been composed in England during the early part of the twelfth century. However, the legend was, without doubt, a very old one, existing long before the Norman poet used it as the framework for his rhyme. Indeed, this poet begins by stating quite clearly that his tale is derived from a British source. An abridged version, based in part upon the French poem, was written by Geoffrei Gaimar, also in the twelfth century. Gaimar claimed that his source had been Gildas, the sixth century Christian monk and that the story may date back to AD500. Other summaries, abridgements and references to the story can also be found in the literature of the Middle Ages. The English versions of the lay had long been given up for lost. Fortunately, however, an English version of the Lay of Havelok, written in rhyming couplets in the Lincolnshire dialect and dating back to AD1280, was eventually found in the Bodleian Library at Oxford in the early part of the nineteenth century.

There have been many theories and commentaries about the Grim legend over the centuries, without doubt, with studies, translations and numerous books appearing, particularly since the re-discovery of the English manuscript. The story has also reappeared in many novel forms, I might add, often sadly based upon the later English version, which has undeniably suffered more changes and hardships, than the earliest available direct account written nearly two centuries earlier.

Professor Skeat managed to collect all known references to the legend at the time he wrote a preface for the Early English Text Society edition of the English lay, published in 1868. In his opinion, this legend was the result of traditional narratives associated with Northumbria and Lindsey, woven round some central Lincolnshire folk hero who had lived in the sixth century. Skeat found it difficult to positively identify Havelok with anyone from recorded history with any degree of certainty, yet he believed that Blecca of Lincoln, baptised by Paulinus, was a possible contender.

Charles Whistler also examined the legend, in greater depth than most. In 1900 he produced the first English novel of Havelok the Dane, extensively based on all the known sources. Whistler has given ample evidence to indicate that – apart from the one instance of the Norman poet substituting the decidedly French name of Argentille for Goldburga – for aesthetic reasons the Norman-French version has retained many names of Northern origin that the English version had lost. The Welsh and even Celtic names and elements have also survived. In a lecture given to the Viking Club in 1902, Whistler showed that his investigations of the texts had convinced him that the Norman poet had been honest about his source having been British:

It seems evident that we have in 'Havelok' a story of Dano-Welsh origin, not so far removed from its original that medievalisation has hidden its salient points. It is a tale of England, but the Saxon element, in the earliest version, is entirely absent, while the Dane and Briton keep their place. It would seem, therefore, to be a traditional Welsh record of actual historic events which occurred in the first unrecorded days of the invasion from the North and the East which followed the retreat of Rome from our shores, when the British princelings yet held their own for a time throughout the land. Havelok may be contemporaneous with Hengist, or earlier, but an actual leader of a Danish force, and holder of a throne at Lincoln and in Norfolk, after expulsion of the British prince who held the one, and had regained the other. He may have been a leader of the historic Jutes, and the camps of the Lincolnshire coast may well be his, and his men and Alsi's lie at Tetford. And Grim, his foster father, in the old Northern way, who takes to the craft of the fisher in England, is surely drawn from life, and may without doubt be held as the actual founder of the town we know. Beyond this, no date can well be assigned. That the tale belongs distinctly and solely to our island seems to prove that it is not old, as Sagas go; but whether the Danes taught it to the Welsh, or whether it is an actual memory of British history may be conjecture. That the hero is a Dane, and that his fortunes involve a British defeat, would go far to show that, as preserved by the Britons, it is a record of fact, and not a mere invention, or echo of far more ancient legend.

Whistler can be remembered as being one of the truly great champions of the Grim story, essentially showing us that ancient legend and romance could be based on historical fact rather than fiction. He can also justly be remembered for bravely going further than most in the matter of dealing with the Arthurian aspects of the tale.

The Norman story, followed by Gaimar, says that the invader and usurper was no other than Arthur of Britain himself, with a subordinate leader of the entirely Scandinavian name of Hodulf, who acts as the tenant for Arthur of the usurped Danish throne. The English poem does not mention this, being content to introduce a dishonest regent instead of a conqueror; but the version which claims to represent the original Welsh has evidently kept the very Welsh mention of Arthur, and probably has also preserved the name of the actual leader of the expedition correctly. Of course the claim for Arthur that he conquered Denmark is old, and generally scouted as impossible. But is it not possible that this half-forgotten story may record the actual expedition which started the claim? There were Danish settlements in Wales, on the Severn Sea, till AD 795, and Danish settlements on the Northumbrian coasts from time immemorial, probably. If a Scandinavian leader gathered a force on our shores, possibly after wintering there, including a Welsh contingent from his neighbours, and made a successful raid thence into Denmark, it would be enough to be remembered and set to the credit of the mighty king, that once a force of Britons were victorious in Denmark.

In *The History of the Kings of Britain*, written around 1136 by Geoffrey of Monmouth, we are informed that Arthur had re-captured Lincoln and York from the Saxons in the sixth century and had, indeed, later made an invasion and conquest of Denmark. It is still possible that Grim may have been contemporaneous with Arthur of Britain. Although the earliest Norman-French versions only make brief, matter-of-fact references to Arthur, it is enough to indicate that the legend may hold definite historical clues to other major traditional accounts. In turn, it may not be surprising to find, on examination, new evidence and clues to the truth behind the legend of Grim and Havelok actually emerging from other isolated, minor legendary accounts.

Yet there has been great confusion, controversy and conflict of opinion concerning this legend. When it has been taken seriously, enthusiasm to find recorded potential identities for Grim and Havelok has given rise to claims and counter-claims that these characters could have lived at any time between the sixth and eleventh centuries. Clearly something is amiss.

We know that in the early part of the fourteenth century, the people of Lincoln were convinced that the old, traditional tale had been based on historical fact. For example, Robert Manning of Bourne (in Lincolnshire), wrote that there was a strong tradition surviving in Lincoln whereby visitors were shown the actual boulder Havelok is said to have thrown when competing for Goldburga's hand, as well as the chapel site where he and she were allegedly wed. Curiously enough, by the seventeenth century, the people of Grimsby appear to have inherited a centuries old tradition and had claimed possession of 'Havelok's Stone' (Figure 2) for themselves.

We cannot be sure that the burgesses of the town had the boulder bestowed upon them centuries before, yet according to the seventeenth century Grimsby antiquarian, Gervase Holles, it had long been used as a boundary marker separating the borough of

Figure 2. 'Havelok's Stone', Welholme Galleries, Grimsby. *www.stonefree.org*

Grimsby from the parish of Wellow, and it has always been known locally as Havelok's Stone. Since no trace of the original stone can be found within the castle grounds at Lincoln, it appears that the later claim may be genuine.

Bluestones

Grimsby has retained two bluestones, or 'blewstones' from its ancient past, both of which have always been vaguely associated with Grim, Havelok and the legend. Although they have been described as bluestones by historians over the centuries, only one is a true bluestone – the one known as Havelok's Stone is actually pink granite. Although both have been used as boundary markers in the past, it is only the bluestone that has featured on old maps of the town.

The mysterious old bluestone of Grimsby sat quietly upon the open sea marsh common ground near to the old haven entrance for centuries, and appears to have had the town grow and develop around it. It was never known who may originally have placed the stone at that site or, indeed, whether it was just a glacial boulder deposited there naturally. The bluestone was only officially designated as a parish boundary marker early in the nineteenth century in order to settle disputes arising between the freemen of Grimsby and the people of Clee over the rights to use the common for pasture. From investigations into the Grim and Havelok legend during the last two years, a discovery has been made that may throw new light upon the origin of this ancient stone and how it came to its site.

In the early 1820s, around the time when the English written version was discovered amid great excitement at Oxford, unbeknown to the academics a discovery was also being made independently near North Thoresby in Lincolnshire. Historian Henry Evans Smith, from Caistor in Lincolnshire, learned from conversations with several elderly rustics at the village of Audby, situated eight miles south-west of Grimsby, that they had also inherited an old, traditional legend concerning a man named Grim.

They said that their Grim and his man, Boundel, had been in Lindsey long before the Viking invasions. Grim had been a giant of a fellow, as was Boundel, and a seafarer, captain of a ship he sailed widely on trading missions. When famine and drought stole over the land, Grim and Boundel sailed across to Denmark and stole two magic ancient bluestones from the king and brought them back to Lindsey, landing at Tetney Haven. They then set up these bluestones at croft sites at Audby and North Thoresby. Here the stones should have remained, serving as focal points for ceremony, feasting, rituals and much more. Yet, after a number of years, Grim's Stone (Figure 3) – which had been used to make the corn grow – suddenly vanished. Boundel's Stone (Figure 4) had been used to bring rain.

Could the mysterious bluestone of Grimsby actually be Grim's Stone? There is a real possibility that this isolated, orally preserved tradition has survived reasonably intact due to association with the famine and the ancient stones. It may be that Grim, the seafarer of the North Thoresby legend, could be the selfsame hero later found

Figure 3. This mysterious ancient bluestone may be 'Grim's Stone', brought back from Denmark in the sixth century. *www.stonefree.org*

Figure 4. Kevin Gracie and Roy 'Stone' Naylor rediscover the 'magical' Boundel's Stone at North Thorseby. *www.stonefree.org*

saving the life of Havelok, before fleeing to England and founding the town of Grimsby. Perhaps, after the famine had passed, there came a time when Grim saw fit to return quietly for the magic Danish bluestone for his new settlement, Grimsby.

When a classic British folk-heroic tale has the ability to run the gauntlet of time and survive more than a thousand years, being described as a myth, legend, romance, fairy tale and fable, it is not surprising that, from local folklore, one finds the irresistible but vital magic ingredient needed to establish the fact that, regardless of all else, there really was a remarkable man named Grim.

Notes and References

1 Lindsey was a sixth century kingdom between the Humber Estuary in the north, and the Fenlands and the River Witham in the south. There were marshlands and sea to the east, and the flood plains of the Trent to the west. Lincoln was its capital.

2 *The Saga Book of the Viking Club*, Volume III, Part III (published in January 1904).

3 As Tetford is the legendary site of the great battle fought in Lindsey to gain the princess her kingdom, the seven ancient burial mounds that exist there may hold clues and evidence of that battle, and tribute to warriors of both camps.

Acknowledgements

I would like to respectfully thank my friend and colleague, Roy 'Stone' Naylor for photography and digital imaging work. I would also like to pay tribute to Ethel Rudkin, the Lincolnshire folklorist, whose efforts during the last century have resulted in the preservation of the North Thoresby legend.

5. THE HUMBER KEELS

by Karen Prescott

KEELS WERE MULTI-PURPOSE cargo carriers that were unique to, and saw service on, the River Humber until after the turn of the twentieth century. One survivor of those golden days in the keel, *Comrade* (Figure 1), which is approximately 250 years old.

Figure 1. *Comrade,* a Humber keel, under sail in July 2000. *Humber Keel & Sloop Preservation Society*

Restored by the Humber Keel & Sloop Preservation Society, *Comrade* can now be seen sailing the Humber once more, her keel cutting easily through the glistening water just as it did centuries before. But, today, the old workhorse is used for an entirely different purpose, as a pleasure craft.

Waterway carriers
Each with a single mast, a square sail and bluff-bowed hulls, the Humber keels were descendants of medieval trading vessels that carried cargoes more than five hundred years ago. However, unlike these medieval craft that tended to rely solely on the wind for sailing power, keels could also navigate inland waterways as well as coastal, sailing such rivers as the Don and Humber. Also, canals were being built on a large scale in the eighteenth century due to the industrial revolution creating better waterways and navigation for transportation. It was because the keels were ideally suited to these waterways that they survived well into the twentieth century.

Towards the end of the nineteenth century, an average keel measured approximately sixty-one feet (18.6 metres) in length, and fifteen feet (5.2 metres) in width, with a draft of around six feet (1.8 metres). A good strong wind blowing in the right direction and into the huge, square sail powered these vessels, especially on open coastal areas such as the Humber, meant they could carry their cargoes into the heart of industrial Yorkshire. Without the aid of wind power, however, they would encounter some difficulty. This was particularly the case on canals where the narrowness of the waterway made it difficult for them to tack to the wind.

At these times, keel owners would use alternative methods of propulsion. Owners tended to work together as a family unit, so when there was no wind, one method was to have someone on shore, hauling by hand. This was usually a woman of the keelfolk. She would walk the towpath with a harness around her shoulders and upper arms, to which one end of a rope was attached. The rope's other end was tied to the front of the keel, thus enabling her to tow the vessel along behind her. This task was not as horrendous as it appears, because once the keel was moving on water its weight was very light.

Meanwhile, the man of the keel family would have remained aboard setting the sail in an attempt to catch as much wind as possible. There were also other craft sailing the canals so it was important to keep a distance from them – therefore the woman tended to feel she had the safer job, ashore.

Another method of propulsion, also usually undertaken by the woman, was known as 'pushing'. This involved propelling the keel along with a boat hook – a pole approximately fifteen feet in length and three inches diameter, with an iron claw at one end. The process of pushing looked very similar to punting, but due to the immense difference in the size of a keel compared to a punt, it was extremely slow and tiring work. Also, from time to time, the pole tended to snap and the pusher would fall into the canal.

The easiest, quickest and safest alternative was using the horse marine service. This involved hiring a man and his horse to tow the keel, but they had to be booked in advance. As the keelfolk were working class people, money was short, so their preferred method of propulsion was one that was carried out free-of-charge, by a woman.

Water gypsies

Because the keelfolk earned their living carrying multi-purpose cargoes back and forth over the Humber they came to be regarded by some members of society as 'water gypsies'. It is quite easy to understand why – they had very introverted natures and led a free lifestyle that paralleled Romany life on land.

Keels also represented old Romany caravans. Made from wood and with a large sail, they were similar to the caravan with its canvas cover. Inside, the cabin area was also set out in a similar style to the Romany caravan. It was situated at the rear of the vessel and entered from a hatchway on the deck via a vertical ladder. Inside the cabin, there was only about six feet of headroom which was then reduced in the centre by a hefty wooden beam that went from one side of the keel to the other. Its purpose was to support the deck above. In its centre hung a paraffin lamp, the only means of illumination, apart from three small portholes to the deck above.

Children were born and bred aboard the keels, and it was in the cabin area where the majority of family life took place. At the front of the cabin was a stove with an open coal fire, an oven and a water boiler. As there was no running water for drinking, cooking, or washing on board, it had to be brought down the vertical ladder, in buckets, from the water barrels stored on deck. Over the stove was a mantelpiece where, apparently, a good quality clock always took pride of place. Above the clock hung a calendar and a tide table.

The other three sides of the cabin were mostly taken up with cupboards. Two large ones on either side concealed two double beds, whilst the others held items such as food, crockery, clothing and fuel – everything needed to maintain a family. On the same three sides, below these cupboards, was more cupboard space with mahogany tops that created a seating area around a central table which was stowed away when not in use.

Even at the end of the nineteenth century, life was run by rules and regulations. Under the *Canal Boats Act* 1877, keels had to be registered as dwelling places with their local authority. This registration specified the maximum number of people allowed to live on board. It also stated that a cabin occupied by a husband and wife could not also be occupied by a girl of twelve, or a boy above the age of fourteen.

Sadly, by the turn of the twentieth century, after the keels had carried their cargoes for approximately two hundred years, the rapid growth of industrialisation created better road and railway systems bringing about a decline in the use of these vessels. Although a few remained in use up to the mid-twentieth century, the majority were either sold as houseboats or scrapped.

This great drop in the need for keels came as a massive blow to the keel community. It also had a drastic knock-on effect on other water-based industries, such as sailmakers, ship chandlers, boat builders and repairers. Their lifestyle and means of employment, as they had known it, became virtually non-existent, forcing them to look for alternatives. Families could no longer work together, and sons were no longer able to take over from their fathers. Many keelfolk turned to working down the pits that were springing up all over South Yorkshire, or in the mills. They had lost their freedom as well as their vessels.

A survivor

Fortunately, one of these historical multi-purpose cargo carriers, that had also seen service on, and was unique to, the Humber, has managed to survive. This is because a Hull engineer, Cedric Lodge, realising how Humber sailing craft were becoming extinct, was instrumental in forming the Humber Keel & Sloop Preservation Society in 1970. Its purpose: to restore and preserve some of these wonderful vessels.

On 16 December 1974, the Society took ownership of the keel *Comrade,* with the intention of re-rigging and restoring her – preserving this approximately 250 year old craft for future generations (Figure 2). In the hustle and bustle of today's materialistic world, we appear to live life at a much faster pace than our ancestors, but fortunately *Comrade* still works at a more serene level, even though the nature of her work is entirely different from that of her old life.

Figure 2. *Comrade,* in full sail. *Humber Keel & Sloop Preservation Society*

Comrade is stored and maintained during the winter at Beverley Beck in East Yorkshire, and is sailed to South Ferriby in the spring, ready to give visitors an opportunity to step back in time and sail with her during the warmer months along her old, familiar path of the Humber.

The Humber Keel & Sloop Preservation Society is a registered charity that owns other antique craft, restored and in top condition, all working now as pleasure boats instead of pack horses. Further information can be obtained on 01652 635288.

6. THE DROWNED VALLEY

by Ray Carey

IT TOOK THE CATASTROPHIC floods of the winter of 2001 to excite the interest of the general public in schemes that involved something as mundane as land drainage. But flood prevention, however costly, is unlikely to need innovative engineering. Contrast this with the impact of the Ancholme valley drainage scheme of 1634-41 – in terms of engineering challenges and work, it not only dominated its era but could be said to be the largest corporate work since the building of the monasteries, paralleled only by a similar scheme on North Lincolnshire's Isle of Axholme. But how did it affect the people?

A scheme that should have benefited them, despite the loss of large parts of their improved common land, proved to be of profit to only a few. Although for many there was gainful work to be had, there was also active and covert resistance that not only heralded the coming of the Civil War, but also probably increased the number of supporters of Parliament against the King.

The story of this scheme focuses upon South Ferriby. It was here that the Adventurers established their working headquarters, and it was the site of an engineering marvel of the era: the Great Sluice (Figure 1).

Figure 1. Ferriby Sluice c.1920. In the foreground is the swing bridge that crossed the Sluice navigation lock until it was replaced, in the 1980s, with today's motorised drawbridge. Top left is the *Hope and Anchor* pub which can be dated from before 1800, but the building in the top centre probably dates back to the 1750s when the ruined Monson Sluice of 1638 was finally replaced. *Pauline Heathershaw collection*

About 800 square kilometres of North Lincolnshire are drained through the part of the Ancholme valley that extends from Bishopsbridge, near Lincoln, to the Humber at South Ferriby. Until the 1630s, the 20,000 or so acres of below-Humber-tide-levels relied on the ancient, embanked wending channel of the old River Ancholme for drainage, the waterway upon which many vessels ferried goods and people. Indeed, before the advent of well-surfaced roads, the River Ancholme was the only option for movement for greater parts of the year.

Most of the old river has disappeared with the introduction of man-made drainage, but its continuing role as the boundary of the parishes of the Valley ensures that its memory lives on.

The problem needed solving

> *...refight the violente and tempestuous rage of the watters of Humbre...*

These words, found in a report of the local Commission of Sewers of 1576, highlight the continued attempts of the committee fronting the Ancholme Valley to win back their levels[1] after about thirty years of depredation from the Humber. A plaint to the crown in 1578 stated that:

> *...the great River of Humber had then so worne away the medowes and comen pasture grondes of the said towne of South Ferryby that within the space of thirtie or forty yeares last past your said subjectes had wasted and consumed their goodes in making and mainteyninge of their banckes ther to their utter impoverishinge and undoinge...*

There was at least one attempt, ordered by a Commission of 1576, to improve the situation, but it is clear that, by the 1630s, the problem still remained to be solved. Unlike today, there was no pressure on 'local government' to improve the lot of their electorate – the power of the common vote did not exist. True, there was a mechanism via the Commission of Sewers where those who would benefit from repairs could be made to share its costs, but it was clear that the customary patching-up of the existing drainage system was inadequate.

A far more ambitious scheme was necessary. But this was a time when any expenditure beyond mere maintenance had doubtful legality. It needed the direct intervention of the only group of people in the Valley with both the power and the stimulus to do something the gentry. Close study of their actions, and the scheme they employed, shows that their motivation was not only to improve the conditions of the level for all – indeed, it was not even the main objective for them – it was a means of obtaining freehold ownership of about a third of the acres of the level, much of it common land or land owned by smaller, less powerful freeholders.

The scheme put forward by a group of gentry Adventurers, led by a local owner, Sir John Monson, aimed at finally draining about 18,000 acres of 'drowned' lands of the Ancholme levels. The price they intended to exact upon landholders was that the Adventurers would gain freehold ownership of 5,827 acres, a third of the reclaimed land. How the Commissioners came to approve this scheme is a story in itself. Here, there is only room to note that, in 1634, use was made of a previous procedure that had circumvented local resistance, by use of Crown decree, in order to effect the drainage of the Isle of Axholme and the flatlands around the Wash. The Crown actively supported such projects, because it stood to profit, at a time when Charles I was desperately in need of funds that had been denied him because he was attempting to rule without Parliament.

The Adventure

> *I sing Floods muzzled and the Ocean tamed, Luxurious Rivers governed and reclaimed...*[2]

The scheme was forced past the many sceptical local people without their assent by the simple procedure of the Commission declaring, after survey, that all would have to contribute a swingeing amount for draining of each of their drowned acres, knowing full well that the demands would be ignored. Once the Commission could declare a failure to collect the required amount, a group willing to take on the job could be employed. Successful completion would mean that this group would be 'paid', by being given freehold ownership of a proportion of the drained acres.

The survey report and its accompanying map, made by Francis Wilkinson of Wrawby, were presented in March 1635. A jury of the Commission, made up of representatives from each of the Ancholme-side communities, reported on the state of their levels plus who controlled their lordships, together with a note of other freeholders. Already they had stated that:

> *...by the inquisition and verdict of John Downes of Horkstow, Gentleman [the foreman of the jury] and other his fellows of the jury*

*of Sewers for the River Ancholme, that carres marshes and feeding
grounds – are and have been for many years hurtfully surrounded
and of late years more than heretofore by reason of defects in the said
river – and for want of a sufficient Sluice or Clowe near the outfall of
the said river.*

Much later, it was to be claimed by the people of Winterton, who
were in strong opposition to the scheme, that the Commission's jury
was made up of *men of weak understanding and small estates...* and that
the Commission was *both commisioners, and undertakers, judges and
parties....* The latter was, undoubtedly, true because it can be shown
that the majority of the Adventurers were drawn from the
Commission as well as being principal Lords of the Ancholme valley
communities.

South Ferriby was an exception to this because its entry in the
survey states that *Mr Michaell Reniger was Chiefe Lord of that psh*
[parish] *and is laitely deceased and hath left eight daughters....* In fact,
the parish register reveals that Michael Reniger, Rector and Lord of
the Manor, and his wife Anne, had been buried in May 1634 leaving
eight daughters, all under eighteen years of age. No doubt the lack
of a lord would have reduced any influence the village might have put
upon the Commission, but there must have been general support, for
the scheme was in their interests. Certainly, South Ferriby's 'price'
was to be the loss of a much smaller proportion of their levels than
most other communities. The Adventurers were to enclose only 20
acres of the 324 (six per cent) that had been adjudged as *hurtfully
surrounded*. This compares with Horkstow's 77 acres of 270 (28 per
cent) and Saxby All Saint's 351 acres of 1,122 (32 per cent).

Returning to the South Ferriby entry, the content of the second
part is typical of that for other communities, in that it describes the
extent of the hurt: *That Lordship hath divers lands overflowed by the
Salte water*, but finishes with a phrase: *...the wch doth litle harme*,
which, intriguingly enough, has been lined through. This may have
been an attempt to give a more favourable slant towards the
drainers' case; several of the entries for other parishes are similarly
altered.

Of the two tenders received, Sir John Monson's was accepted. He
was a major landowner in Lincolnshire, with estates bordering the
south part of the levels. The only other bid came from what he
described as a group of *furraigners* who wanted nearly half of the
drained land as their price, compared to the one third required by Sir
John's group.

The Anderson Accounts

Much of the progress and technical detail of the construction phase has been gleaned from an invaluable account of the expenditure and income involved that is in the care of Lincolnshire Archives Office as part of the Monson deposit. It was compiled by Robert Anderson of Broughton, the man appointed by the Adventurers as *expenditur of all monies and overseer of the works.*

Anderson was a junior member of an Adventure family who were Lords of Broughton, and he described himself as 'cousin' of Francis Frobisher, gentleman of South Ferriby. Since his presence was required at the South Ferriby office and stores built by the Adventurers, it seems likely that he lodged with his cousin at North Grange for the duration of the scheme.

He records every penny that was collected and received. The scheme was financed in several phases with each Adventurer paying regular 'layes' of five shillings (25p) per acre for the portion of acres for which he had contracted. In all, six and a half layes were collected to produce the £9,466 needed to finance the project. Only by comparing the known wage rates for labourers working on the project with today's rates can we make a very approximate modern comparison of the cost – about £14 million. Labourers could expect about 9d (4½p) per day and, between them, they earned nearly £4,000 – which must have had a dramatic affect upon the economy of the valley communities, including pushing up farm labouring rates.

Somewhere around 15,000 man-weeks was paid for, making an average workforce of about 150. But by far the highest levels of labour for the thirty-month project are found in the summer of 1637 when, for seven months, there was an average workforce of approximately 240, peaking to 340 in the August.

Of the skilled workers, the stonemasons were highest paid, at about two shillings per day (10p) whilst, of the surprisingly small management team, Mr Hill, the engineer, received the most at £4 per week, and Robert Anderson, £2.

The cost of completing the Sluice cannot be accurately calculated because some expenses were often hidden in those other items; but the diary of Abraham de la Pryme of Broughton, written some fifty years later, claimed that the figure was £3,000. Clearly, what was an enormous overall sum for its time, came in well above budget because two of the investors pulled out before completion, thus forfeiting their acres.

Central to Mr Hill's design was the cutting of the New River, an

eighteen mile straight drain that was to be six feet (1.8 metres) deep
and about forty feet (12.2 metres) wide from the centre of the levels
from Kingerby, near Bishops Bridge, to a 'state of the art' sluice at
the valley's interface with the River Humber at South Ferriby. Close
study of maps and records of the time shows that the New River was
designed to pick up the River Rase at Kingerby, and all other
drainage south of Brigg. The old river between Brigg and the ancient
four-arched bridge at Ferriby was widened and deepened to carry
drainage from the levels north of Brigg and discharge, as it always
had, through a clow or sluice at the bridge.

One feature, an innovation for its time, was the construction of
side drains to intercept the water before it could enter the levels,
carrying it into the main drains further downstream. The use of a
series of side clews (sluices) and tunnels, particularly at Scabcroft
in Winterton, integrated the system. This design meant that the
legal requirement to maintain a passageway for vessels from the
Humber was upheld by continuing to use the old river, at least as
far as Brigg.

The most impressive part of the works was the sluice built at the
outfall of the New River, and it must, for its time, have been an
advanced piece of engineering. We know that Mr Hill, the engineer,
had constructed a model of it because Anderson paid out 6d (2¹/₂p)
for a pownde of glew to make the modell of the sluice... and on 20 August
1636, a shilling was given *to William Stamford for caryinge and
recaryinge the model of the Sluce.* The latter, no doubt, was for its
journey to be examined by the Adventurers at their regular meeting
place, *The Angel* public house, Brigg.

Hill's design was, for its time, an ingenious solution to the age-old
problem of draining levels that had so little gradient throughout their
eighteen-mile length to the Humber. It should have been effective, as
was noted in a 1759 report by the most eminent drainage engineers
of their time, John Smeaton and John Grundy, who thought that the
Hill design had been planned *in masterly manner...* However, as will
be shown, the disruption of the works that followed soon after their
completion means that it was never given the opportunity of
practical proof.

The wide search for timber
Anderson's account lists visits all over northern Lincolnshire and
Yorkshire in search of timber and stone; indeed, the former was soon
to be brought from woods in Broughton, Appleby, Crowle, Hurst
and Seaton (Yorkshire), and firwood was sought from as far south as

Figure 2. Ferriby Sluice with Rugby Cement works in the background, viewed from the Humber side of the sluice that was built in 1830 to replace the eighteenth century version. The main difference is that a separate canal, which left the main river via a staunch about 1,000 metres inland, served the navigation lock of the earlier version. Today's lock is part of the main sluice. Careful study of maps and contemporary documents site the sluice of 1638 close to the white boat that appears in the right of this photograph. *Pauline Heathershaw collection*

Spalding, Lynne and Boston in south Lincolnshire. But so much timber was needed for the scheme, that wood was eventually brought to Hull from Scandinavia and rafted over the Humber to Ferriby's old haven, in July.

The huge quantities of timber and the numbers of wheelbarrows – at least 220 – that had to be purchased indicate the techniques employed in cutting the New River and other drains. After digging and barrowing, the cut must have been side-shored throughout with timber, but the sluice pit was to be lined with brick and stone, its bottom piled with timber from Redings Wood, south of Brigg. The biggest challenge must have been to make the massive sluice doors work – doors that la Pryme was to claim needed a cart and eight horses to move each of them ...*by reason of the great quantity of ironwork that was there.*

The most notable item that appears in the Anderson accounts is the purchase, in London, of specially made brassware for hinges and bottom runners *for the gates to run in...* for the large sum of £123. South Ferriby's blacksmith, Thomas Trippe, must have done well out of the work judging by the amount of *grate spikes*, nails, *spanish iorn* and wheelbarrow spindles that were bought from him, as well as the work for which he was paid at the Sluice.

Much of the later ironwork came from blacksmiths at Barton and Kirton-in-Lindsey, who presumably could produce the more specialised requirements.

The final comment about materials is saved for brickwork and cement, because it was bricks, tiles and a working sluice that were to transform the fortunes of nineteenth century South Ferriby – as much as making cement from the limestone in the hill has done for today's village. Proof that brickmaking was not a village occupation before this time is to be found in Anderson's accounts. The first purchase of bricks came from a house in Barton-upon-Humber that was bought and then demolished, *chymneys* and all, to be used for the construction of the offices and yard that served the sluice site.

However, local arrangements were being planned because the fee of two shillings was paid in August *to a brickmaker that came to Broughton and Fereby*, presumably to assess the clay. By November, his work must have been in full swing, because he is paid nearly £78 for making *90 thousand and ode hundredes of Brickes*, at least some of which were probably made in Ferriby from the same clay areas near today's sluice that were used in the nineteenth century.

As for the making of cement, there are payments for chalders[3] of 'Feriby Lyme' which must have come from the hillside overlooking the main village. However, the site of the only kiln that is mentioned is Brigg, although the building of a chimney at the sluice using bricks from the demolished Barton house may have been connected to this as well as brickmaking.

A study of the surnames of people who were paid for key roles, such as leading (carting) the many loads of materials, reveals names of South Ferriby families such as the Brombies, Scarboroughs and Waddinghams. As well as the blacksmith, Thomas Trippe, Anderson's cousin, Frobisher, is paid for sledding stone in the sluice area.

Inevitably, problems caused delays in completion of the project. For example, in October 1636, the work was affected by a great storm and tide that broke the new sea bank and damaged the sluice gates. Later, there was a major collapse of a dam in Horkstow. But the main problem was local resistance to the scheme. As early as 13 July in the first year, there is payment for *a messenger – sent to Sir John Monson when Sir John Wrayes men threw earth into the new river.*

Sir John Wray, Lord of Winterton, became one of the main Lincolnshire supporters of Parliament in the Civil War. His latter role may have had some significance, because it is generally accepted now that the drainage project drew many local sufferers to the side of Parliament in reaction to what was seen as the highhandedness of the Crown in encouraging and profiting from such adventures.

But what we can learn, from a case surrounding the Adventurers' attempts to reclaim their Winterton enclosures after the years of ruin and neglect of the Civil War, shows that it was the yeomen and commoners who kept up their active resistance to the scheme.

The final outcome

> *Behold the great design, which they do now determine,*
> *Will make our bodies pine, a prey to crows and vermin;*
> *For this they do mean all fens, and waters overmaster...*[4]

As for the fate of the 'Great Adventure' – as soon as the Civil War was underway, Sir John Monson claimed that the sluice was damaged by the men of Winterton, and that he was

> *...kept out of Possession above twenty years, notwithstanding his great expence; and by it destroyed his Works and Sluces, for want of repairing them, as it may cost him ten thousand pound to recover and perfect the Work.*

He managed to restore the scheme for a short while in 1662, only to see the sluice broken by the Winterton men who, he claimed, supported their case with guns and other weapons. He, and the other Undertakers, continued to enjoy the freeholds they had won, largely from the commoners and small owners, but the levels remained undrained until the 1760s. A study of the rent and sale prices of the acres in the late seventeenth century shows that, despite the complete failure of their scheme, the Adventurers were well in pocket by that time, despite their failure to drain the valley.

A map of 1667 reveals more land worn off at the Humber frontage, a fact confirmed by the land deeds of the period that reveal large areas of the raised cliff at the northern end of South Ferribly, adjacent to the Humber, had gone for ever. These effects may actually have resulted from the cutting of the New River and sluice. If, as seems likely, a bank of mud, flushed through the outfall from the works, was formed in the Humber, then this may have focused the tides that eroded both the frontage and the raised cliff at the north end of the parish. Certainly, the next known phase of major erosion in this area started soon after a scheme in the 1800s that involved widening and deepening the New River.

De la Pryme's notes of 1680 confirm the continuing ruin of Ferriby's Sluice, and the later report by William Stukely is final testament to its fate, as well as the long-lasting affect it must have had upon the village. Stukely records his visit in 1724 in Itenerarium Curiosum:

> *We passed by the spring of old Winteringham and the marsh at the mouth of the river Ankam, which is a vast track of land left by the sea and come to Ferriby Sluice, a stately bridge of three arches with sluices for the avoidance of water escaping into the sea, but now broken down and lying dismally in ruins by negligence of the undertakers.*

After a graphic description of his passage across the river: *in a paltry short boat commanded by a little old deaf fellow with a long beard,* he found *several clayey lakes to ride over impasseable in Winter,* before arriving at the village on the hillside which he described as: *a sorry ragged place where upon the stocks is wrote 'fear God Honour the King'.*

The overall effect of the Great Adventure which, for a few years, produced a prosperous boom town at the very frontiers of contemporary technology, was to leave it 'a sorry ragged place' with shrinking population, a ruined sluice, tide-drowned levels and even fewer surviving Ings and Groves than before. So it remained, until the 1760s, when the first of several attempts to repair the sluice and drain the valley led to the work of the Rennies in the 1800s. They were able to solve the problem permanently, and bring to Ferriby Sluice and the village on the hill the burgeoning prosperity of its brickyards.

Notes and References

1 Levels – tracts of land of uniform elevation.
2 Samuel Fortrey, 1685.
3 Chalders – chaldrons, i.e. units of dry measure equal to 32 to 36 bushels.
4 Anon verse by fenmen of the time, from Samuel Smiles, *The Lives of Engineers* (1861-62).

Space does not permit of the multiplicity of footnotes that would be needed to detail the sources used for this chapter – which is no more than a brief summary of a complete work by the author on the history of the Ancholme Levels that is awaiting publication.

Acknowledgements

The bulk of the information came from the Monson family papers stored at Lincolnshire Archives Office. Grateful acknowledgement is due to the trustees of the 10th Lord Monson for ensuring that this wealth of papers pertaining to the case have survived to embellish the history of our county. This work would not have been possible without the careful stewardship by Lincolnshire Archives Office of the many documents used, and also the patient guidance of its staff. Thanks also to Pauline Heathershaw of South Ferriby for the use of photographs from *South Ferriby – A 4000 Year Odyssey.*

Bibliography

The Diaries of Abraham de la Pryme, Surtees Society, 54 (1870).
Itenerarium Curiosum, Second Edition; London, Baker and Leigh.

7. THE CLEETHORPES PROMENADES

by Alan Dowling

THAT WELL-KNOWN SONG extolling the delights of seaside
holidays contains the significant phrase: 'I do like to stroll along the
prom, prom, prom'. Indeed, one of the pleasures of being 'beside the
seaside' is a relaxed stroll along the promenade, watching the world
go by 'beside the sea'. However, it was not ever so, and our seaside
promenades are a comparatively modern development that we tend
to take for granted. The Cleethorpes promenades are a case in point.
They stretch along the seafront for more than a mile and are a major
feature of the resort. Built in two stages, the North and Central
promenades were completed in 1885; the King's Parade, usually
referred to as the Kingsway promenade, was completed in 1906.
Now an important part of the town's physical heritage, their history
tells us a great deal about the development of the resort.

In the eighteenth century, the main industries in Cleethorpes were
agriculture and inshore fishing. The town was also frequented in the
summer as a bathing resort, and was referred to in 1791 as 'the best
of the Lincolnshire bathing shops'. It grew slowly as a bathing place
during the early nineteenth century, but it was the construction of
the Manchester, Sheffield and Lincolnshire Railway (MS&LR) that
led to its expansion into a significant Victorian seaside resort.

The railway reached nearby Grimsby in 1848 and, although the
line was not at that time extended the further short distance to
Cleethorpes, it still opened up a vast catchment area of potential
visitors from the industrial regions of South Yorkshire, East
Lancashire and the Midlands. They were soon coming in trainloads
to Grimsby, then making their way to Cleethorpes by road transport
or on foot to enjoy the sands, the bathing, the fresh air and the sea
views. However, it was the two and a quarter miles extension of the
railway from Grimsby to the resort in 1863 that resulted in an
accelerated increase of summer visitors and in the town's residential
population and housing stock. This, in turn, led to Cleethorpes
becoming a public health district in 1872, and acquiring its first
municipal local authority in the form of an elected Local Board of
Health. Another result was that a group of local landowners and
entrepreneurs formed a company to finance the construction of a

pleasure pier, which was opened in 1873.

The pier was a popular attraction, providing opportunities for strolls to obtain good prospects of the sea and passing ships, and also to enjoy views of the land on the return journey. But what did these land views reveal? The coastline at Cleethorpes consists largely of boulder clay so the eye was caught mainly by a high but unattractive cliff of clay to the south of the pier. At its highest point, this cliff reached a height of approximately fifty feet (15.2 metres) above the beach and was topped by a rough area of ground divided amongst several owners and tenants and used according to their wishes. These might include growing crops such as cabbages, or holding open-air auctions of marine salvage, including old ropes and ships' timbers. A narrow stretch of land along the top of the cliff was held by the parish for public recreation and accommodated a cliff-top path.

There were calls, from both residents and visitors, for the land at the top of the cliff to be improved and made more attractive. In addition, because the soft cliff was being eroded at an alarming rate, there were calls for a sea wall to be built, to stop both the cliff and the town completely disappearing into the sea. This was not merely a recent occurrence. In 1697, a visiting clergyman recorded that pieces of the cliff as big as churches were being washed away. During the 1870s, the state of the cliffs became a major preoccupation of the new Local Board of Health - in 1875, it was noted that there was a need to protect the cliffs 'from further annihilation' and convert them into a pleasant and attractive promenade. The board investigated the possibility of carrying out a limited scheme of sea defence and improvement but the estimated cost of £14,500 was beyond its pecuniary capabilities. Local major landowners were approached but declined to get financially involved.

The North and Central Promenades
Light appeared on the horizon in 1880 when the MS&LR, after approaches from the Local Board of Health, agreed to provide a sea wall and promenade either side of the pier – that is, the North and Central promenades - and improve the central area of high cliff (Figure 1). A condition of its agreement was that it be allowed to purchase the land at the top of the cliff and, after turning it into pleasure gardens, charge for admission. The MS&LR obtained a private Act of Parliament in 1881 that gave the necessary permission for this work to be undertaken.

Railway shareholders complained at the estimated cost of £33,000, but the company chairman, Sir Edward Watkin, argued that

Figure 1. A view of Cleethorpes seafront, *c.*1880, before the Central and North promenades were completed in 1885. *Grimsby Central Library*

since the line had been extended to Cleethorpes in 1863, the number of passengers carried to the resort by their railway had increased from 41,000 in 1864 to 407,000 in 1881. He maintained that this made the outlay worthwhile. He also stressed that they were 'spending the money to protect the property from the sea and to make the place more attractive'. He then emphasised the long-term commercial importance of the capital outlay to shareholders, in that it meant they would have 'a watering place of their own where they could put all the profits into their own pockets'.

He must have been persuasive, because another Act of Parliament was obtained, in 1884, which permitted further expenditure of £10,000 to provide such visitor attractions as a swimming baths, shops and refreshment rooms. The company also took a lease on the pier and incorporated it into its grand design for the promenade and gardens; it purchased the pier outright in 1904. By the end of the nineteenth century, the MS&LR had invested about £100,000 in resort improvements at Cleethorpes.

The improvement works, which were planned and carried out by engineer and contractor H B James, began in 1883 and, on 2 July 1885, the North and Central promenades and cliff top gardens were officially opened by Prince Albert Victor, the eldest son of the Prince of Wales. That day's celebrations, concluding with a firework display in the evening, were in order because the work had comprehensively transformed the seafront and laid the foundation for yet a further rapid increase in the popularity of the resort.

The present promenades are still essentially as they were when completed in 1885. They were built by constructing an outer wall of masonry blocks on the beach and then filling in the space between it and the shore or, particularly in the case of the Central promenade, the face of the cliff, effectively reducing the apparent height of the cliff. Part of the filling used was furnace slag brought by rail from Scunthorpe ironworks.

The North promenade stretches from the very northern part of the seafront down to the pier and then continues as the Central promenade culminating at the Brighton Street slipway. When constructed, it ran underneath the pier, which joined land at the cliff top. Both promenades feature a wide pedestrian parade, a separate vehicular road and a pavement. Despite their similarity in basic design, each promenade has a distinctive character, partly due to the local topography.

The railway line enters the resort from the north, hugs the coastline and terminates before reaching the higher ground of the central cliff. As part of the improvement works, the original railway station was replaced by a new structure several yards nearer the promenade.[1] Consequently, the packed railway excursions could spill out their passengers within a few yards of the North promenade and the beach. This promenade did not have the adjacent space, high cliff or scenic potential of the Central promenade, so the strip of land between it and the railway line was used for seaside stalls and attractions. Not surprisingly, this area and its beach became popular with day-trippers and, even today, retains stereotypical seaside brashness epitomised by noisy amusement arcades, beach rides, stalls and other diversions.

The Central promenade had scenic possibilities. The high but crumbling cliff was smoothed out and planted as a pleasure garden. The pier entrance was merged into this and a common entrance served both the gardens and the pier. The division between the two promenades was, and is, marked by a new road, Sea Road, which the railway company constructed to replace the rough track that had hitherto led down to the beach. The design of this wide road that served as an impressive approach to the company's improvements illustrated a twofold purpose. The left hand side of the road led straight down to the promenade and beach, while the right hand side curved up to the right as a carriage road leading to the entrance to the pier and the cliff-top gardens. In contrast to the North promenade, the attractions on the Central promenade were of a different nature. An indoor salt-water swimming baths, a museum and aquarium, a camera obscura and a tea garden were amongst the diversions catering for more 'respectable' tastes. The high point of the cliff was marked by a folly constructed of rough blocks of chalk, limestone and furnace slag and named Ross Castle after the secretary of the MS&LR. Nearby, a new staircase giving access from the high cliff to the promenade and beach replaced a set of rickety wooden steps.

The Kingsway Promenade

The railway company had successfully provided two promenades with different atmospheres catering for a variety of public tastes. It had also countered the erosion problem of the high cliff. However, as the end of the century approached, severe erosion was being experienced along the coast to the south of the Central promenade. Currently, this may be identified as the stretch of coastline between the Brighton Street slipway and the seafront Leisure Centre. It consisted of more boulder clay cliff with a track along the top, known as Sea Bank Road. This was a much lower cliff than that backing the Central promenade and had none of its scenic potential.[2] Also, a ribbon of houses had been built along the road facing the sea. Therefore, there was no space on the top of the cliff for pleasure gardens such as those set out on the high cliff behind the Central promenade. Such was the degree of erosion, that the houses along the road were in danger of being damaged or swept away. Property owners had faced part of the cliff with timber, but storms in 1897 damaged the facings so, once again, the town was faced with the question of preventing serious erosion.

In 1897 the local authority, by now transmuted into the Cleethorpes Urban District Council (UDC), asked the railway company to construct a southerly extension of its sea wall and promenade. The railway company, which had now become the Great Central Railway (GCR) declined to take on the commitment; financially, it was heavily engaged in constructing a line to London. Compared with the situation in the 1880s, the local authority could now consider undertaking the work itself. The town's population and housing stock had increased rapidly during the 1890s and, by 1901, there were 12, 578 inhabitants – compared with the 1881 figure of 2,840. The greatly increased rateable income accruing to the UDC therefore made heavy capital outlay a feasible consideration.

The council was also interested in developing the southern part of the town, once the separate township of Thrunscoe, which was still largely agricultural land with the sole road access being the rapidly disappearing Sea Bank Road. If this road was improved and protected, it would open up Thrunscoe to both residential and holiday development. The UDC's own particular concern was to acquire an area that could be developed as a pleasure ground, but nothing came of its approach to a farmer requesting land for this purpose. However, there was other suitable land at what would be the southerly limit of the new promenade - an area of about thirty acres of sand dunes and foreshore, used to some extent as golf links. It was part of the local estate of Sidney Sussex College, Cambridge, owner of most of the land in Thrunscoe and Cleethorpes. The college refused to sell the land, but was prepared to lease it to the council. However, the UDC was aware that a modern road would benefit the college if the Thrunscoe farmland was opened up for building, thereby increasing its potential value. So it insisted that, unless the college sold it the land for development into pleasure gardens, it would not build a new sea wall and road.

In 1901 the college finally agreed to sell thirty-three acres of ground consisting of mainly sand dunes, on condition that the council would proceed with its Sea Bank Road improvement scheme (Figure 2). Accordingly, the scheme was included in a general Improvement Bill being submitted to Parliament by the council. The bill received the royal assent in August 1902 and preparatory work began on the sea wall. During the same year and the ensuing winter, Sea Bank Road suffered very serious erosion and, at one point, an inroad was made to within six feet of some of the houses. Horse-drawn vehicles were unable to proceed along the route and a timber footway was constructed over the gap. The improvement work was carried out on the same lines as the railway promenades: an outer wall was built and the gap between it and the cliff edge was filled in, largely with sand and gravel from the beach.

Construction work suffered from storm damage on several occasions. In September 1903, a gale undid much of the work on the sea wall, causing damage to shuttering, scaffolding, construction tramways, groynes and the roadway. Further major damage occurred

Figure 2. Sea Bank Road, 1902, before the construction of the Kingsway promenade in 1906. *Grimsby Central Library*

in January 1905, when a severe north-easterly gale brought the highest tide to the Lincolnshire coast for twenty years. A stretch of about one hundred yards of the new wall was demolished and several houses suffered serious damage.

The major components of the improvement works were to be a promenade thirty feet (9.1m) wide, a road thirty-five feet (10.7m) wide and a parallel length fifteen feet (4.6m) wide that could be used either for a tramway or, alternatively, as a separate promenade for bathchairs, perambulators and bicycles. Electric trams ran from

Grimsby and the line terminated near to Brighton Street slipway, where the new promenade would start. It was intended that the line should be extended to the far end of the promenade. However, the tramway company and the UDC could not agree on a fare structure to cover the extension and negotiations fell through. The projected alternative use of the tramway was forgotten, and it was set out as the linear gardens that still run alongside the road.

The road, given the name Kingsway, and the promenade, King's Parade, was officially opened in July 1906, by Lady Henderson, the wife of the chairman of GCR. On the same day, she also turned the first sod of the dock that was to be built on the Humber estuary at nearby Immingham. From the outset, the Kingsway promenade was regarded by the UDC, and others, as an attraction that would hopefully raise the status of the resort, attracting the more respectable class of holiday visitor to the town, in addition to the day trippers who tended to congregate in the vicinity of the North promenade and the pier. To this end, the UDC decided not to allow any slot machines or similar entertainment on the new promenade, despite being offered tempting rentals by interested parties.

As was expected, the completion of the Kingsway road led to a southerly extension of the town's residential and resort areas. Neighbouring farmland was soon opened up for house building. Development began in 1907 and the first of the new roads was called Queens Parade, complementing the official name of the Kings Parade promenade. The UDC had plans drawn up in 1910 for the recreational development of the acres of sand dunes it had bought from Sidney Sussex College. But it was not until after the First World War that a bathing pool, boating lake and other facilities were constructed and protected by a sea wall, forming what was termed the Thrunscoe Recreation Ground. Another sea wall, commencing south of the boating lake, was constructed during 1929 and 1930. It was called the Marine Embankment and ran for a further mile, culminating at the town's southern boundary with the parish of Humberston.

Central Promenade Refurbishment
With the continued growth of the town and a rising income from municipal rates, the UDC became increasingly confident about taking a positive part in developing the resort, and, financially, was more able to undertake major capital investment. The completion of the Kingsway promenade in 1906 is an early indication of this (Figure 3).

Figure 3. The Kingsway, *c.*1910. *Grimsby Central Library*

In 1909, the UDC then made an unsuccessful approach to purchase the GCR pier, promenade and cliff-top gardens, which became known as the 'pier gardens'.

In 1924, the national grouping of the railway companies took place and the GCR was absorbed into the newly formed London and North Eastern Railway (LNER). The new company was willing to sell its seafront holdings, but the asking price of £60,000 was too high for the UDC to consider. In 1928, the council prepared for further negotiations by including powers to buy the pier, promenades and pier gardens in its *Parliamentary Improvement Act* of that year. Negotiations in 1934-35 produced a reduced LNER figure of £40,000 and the two parties finally agreed on a price of £27,000. By this time, LNER was primarily concerned with making its railway network pay; its seafront holdings were becoming run down and the UDC wanted to improve them.

Figure 4. Central promenade and gardens, *c.*1930. *Grimsby Central Library*

An added impetus to make changes occurred in 1936, when the urban district was granted a royal charter as an incorporated municipal borough, marking the town's municipal 'coming of age' and giving it added status. It also encouraged the improving spirit that was already evident amongst local councillors. Apart from their wish to effect a general upgrading of the Central promenade (Figure 4) and the pier gardens, there were two particular points that concerned them. Firstly, the two main access points to the Central promenade and beach had become unattractive – that is, Sea Road, and what were termed the High Cliff steps. Secondly, access to the pier should be improved; the pier road that ran over the promenade caused obstruction and spoilt the look of the seafront.

The borough council appointed landscape architect, E P Mawson, to re-plan the pier gardens and other areas of the Central promenade.[3] The estimated cost of the scheme he submitted was

£17,200 and his proposals received general support. By mid-1939, work had been completed on altering and widening Sea Road, taking away the overhead approach to the pier, creating a new pier entrance at promenade level, constructing a new set of High Cliff steps, and replacing the refreshment rooms opposite the pier with a public house. In addition, a strip of land was taken from the landward side of the pier gardens, in order to widen and improve Alexandra Road, which lies behind the gardens and parallel to the Central promenade. More work, due to begin in the autumn, consisting of improving the layout for the pier gardens and providing a new café, kiosks, public conveniences and a car park, was put on hold due to the outbreak of the Second World War.

During the war, a section of the pier was removed by the military as an anti-invasion measure. Post-war, the council decided to demolish the stretch of pier that remained on the seaward side of the gap, reducing the pier to its present length – only a quarter of its original 1,200 feet (417.6 metres). The present pier pavilion was built in 1904 to replace an earlier one, that had stood at the seaward end of the pier until destroyed by fire the previous year. Improvement work, carried out in the seafront area after the war, included using Mawson's plans in the construction of two bow-fronted kiosks at the base of the gardens.

Conclusion

The construction of the North and Central promenades illustrates the dominant role played by the railway in the nineteenth century expansion of the town as a resort. They were built as a capital investment that would produce more fare-paying passengers and greater profits for the shareholders. The building of the Kingsway promenade, demonstrates how the local government authority began to exert its increasing power and confidence in resort development to, eventually, become the owner of the railway company promenades. As sea walls, the promenades halted serious erosion and damage to property; as visitor attractions, they provided a pleasurable and attractive environment, forming the setting and springboard for a wide range of recreational and holiday facilities. Finally, as examples of nineteenth and twentieth century civil engineering, they dominate the seafront and survive as an important part of the town's physical heritage. Their overall impact was to enable the town to compete successfully in the countrywide growth of the seaside holiday industry, and to expand as both a residential town and holiday resort.

Notes and References

1 The old station now accommodates a public house (No.1 Refreshment Room) and may be seen to the north west of the present station.

2 It is not now apparent that there was a cliff along this stretch. This is because of a change in the level of the beach. The change is partly man-made and partly caused by the natural accretion of wind blown sand.

3 E P Mawson was a successful landscape architect and the son of T H Mawson (1861-1933). The latter had an international reputation as a landscape architect and town planner and had prepared a layout for Cleethorpes' Sidney Park which opened in 1904.

Bibliography

1 *Cleethorpes: the Development of an East Coast Resort* by R W Ambler in E M Sigsworth Ports and Resorts (Hull, 1981).
2 *The Story of Cleethorpes* by Frank Baker (Cleethorpes, 1953).
3 *Great Central, Volume III, 1864-1899* by George Dow (London, 1962).
4 *The New Kingsway and Parade*, supplement to the *Grimsby News*, 13 July 1906.
5 *The Official Programme of* [the] *Opening of* [the] *Promenade and Cliff Gardens* (Cleethorpes, 1885).
6 *The Book of the Lincolnshire Seaside*, David N Robinson, (Buckingham, 1981).

8. CLEETHORPES, THE SEASIDE RESORT

by Joanne Mason

IT IS NO COINCIDENCE that a resort's tourism facilities generally occupy the area between the sea and its urban area. For a seaside holiday is just that – time spent beside the sea. The traditional seaside environment, as we know, it revolves not around the resort as a whole, but in a relatively confined area of foreshore – an area of nearshore waters, beach, promenade and seafront buildings. The holiday atmosphere and traditions have been built around this core seaside resort area.

The foreshore areas of seaside resorts often typify the character of the traditional seaside holiday, representing a transitional zone between 'culture' and 'nature'. It has a fundamental distinction between the resort – with its cultural and community atmosphere, social tone and culturally controlled decorum, and the sea and beach – with their natural environment that may be savage, yet provides sensuous pleasures allowing one to behave and 'undress' naturally. Blending at the foreshore, they provide semi-natural areas such as boating lakes, golf courses, swimming pools and zoos or nature parks, plus entertainment and attractions that are frequently temporary or seasonal by nature such as funfairs, amusements and illuminations. Cleethorpes' foreshore typifies this culture/nature divide.

The foreshore began to develop in the mid 1800s and by the 1950s the whole of the seafront was devoted to fun and pleasure with entertainment and all the fun of the fair. Today, Cleethorpes has a long and varied foreshore providing approximately four miles of promenade and marine walks, attractions, entertainment, natural areas and tourist facilities.

Attraction of the seaside

In the early days of seaside popularity the main attraction was its natural elements. It was during the seventeenth century that the aristocracy and gentry began to visit resorts when the benefits of seawater and fresh sea air were introduced by notable medics, such as Dr Wittie and his promotional campaign for sea bathing in Scarborough. Drinking, and bathing in, the salty water to cure a host

Figure 1. High Cliffe, Cleethorpes in 1861. *Grimsby Reference Library, North East Lincolnshire Council*

of ailments, as well as taking in the fresh sea air, benefited the few visitors who could afford the time and money to indulge themselves. As modesty became an issue, bathing machines waited on the beach to take visitors into the sea where the matron would proceed to 'dip' its passenger under the icy water before returning him or her to the privacy of the carriage. Promenading along Cleethorpes natural cliff top was a daily ritual that was eventually extended out over the sea with the appearance of the pier, the first man-made attraction at Cleethorpes (Figure 1).

As the resort developed, more and more was built to attract visitors, and soon the foreshore provided a variety of entertainment and funfairs for those in pursuit of pleasure. Cleethorpes began to resemble the seaside holiday atmosphere that we know and love and that is etched in many childhood memories: the fun of the fair, Punch and Judy shows, souvenir shops with buckets and spades. Times spent with family and friends at the seaside, come rain or shine, were looked forward to all year.

Development of the foreshore
The Lincolnshire resorts were late to develop compared with other

seaside resorts in England and Wales. In 1791 Lord Torrington had described Cleethorpes as 'three miles of boggy turf to Grimsby'. At this time Cleethorpes was little more than a remote fishing village perched on a cliff with a population of 284, but by the early 1800s, it was slowly becoming a bathing place for the well-to-do. From a slow start, Cleethorpes developed rapidly with demand emanating from Yorkshire and the East Midlands, to rapidly push it up the resort hierarchy during the late eighteenth and early nineteenth centuries.

White's 1826 Directory reported Cleethorpes as 'a bathing place for fashionable county gentility'. For the comfort of its visitors and over-looking the sea, the new *Dolphin Hotel* replaced the *Old Cleethorpes Hotel* in 1820 and lodging houses became available for hire. The village and foreshore changed very little due to the passive activities and pastimes that were of interest to early visitors. It was when the 1846 *Enclosure Act* allotted church wardens two and a half acres of seafront, to be set out as public recreation ground, that changes were set in motion, paving the way for the development of Cleethorpes seafront. The picture of the Royal Gardens, circa 1890 (Figure 2), shows the early seafront promenade and pier, and clearly depicts the area of foreshore between sea and settlement. The promenade was an early amusement for walking and taking the air,

Figure 2. Royal Gardens, Cleethorpes, 1890. *Grimsby Reference Library, North East Lincolnshire Council*

but was also a place to be seen and for meeting other resort guests and general socialising.

Prominent Methodists became local government leaders and were the main driving force in the commercial development of Cleethorpes. They organised events, promoted it as a place to visit, and they brought culture and education to the growing resort. However, there came a time when basic local accommodation and a few bathing machines did not suffice. Further development and investment was required to make the resort successful. Basic infrastructure such as water supply, sanitation, roads, lighting and gardens became necessities for a fashionable seaside bathing place. In 1855, a year after an outbreak of cholera, Cleethorpes had improved sanitation and was claimed to be 'exceedingly healthy', so pleasure trips began to run once again, to what was now a town. 'Goodly companies of ladies and gentlemen are to be seen parading the shore...and the whole plant of bathing machines, donkeys and drivers appear to be in full working order'[1] was reported. Cleethorpes once again 'was one of the most eligible and salubrious bathing places in Lincolnshire'.

As the Industrial Revolution gained pace, the increasing prosperity of the rapidly expanding middle classes motivated them to seek further status by partaking in the fashions and rituals of the wealthy. This coincided with the height of the popularity for the sea-bathing season. Advances in transportation reduced the time and cost of travel, so the prospering middle classes aspired to the seaside holiday as an ideal of a cultured and leisured lifestyle. To accommodate the growing numbers of visitors to the resort, the Manchester, Sheffield and Lincolnshire Railway (MS&LR) Company extended a single track to Cleethorpes in 1863, with an immediate effect – 30,000 people arrived by train to attend the Methodist's annual tea meeting. The following year the MS& L R reported figures of 79,000 ordinary and 72,000 excursion visitors. By 1881, there were 230,000 ordinary and 72,000 excursion visitors travelling by train to Cleethorpes, a town that was growing rapidly and ranking among other top English seaside resorts in population and resort growth.

In 1873, the first major resort facility provision was opened – the 1,200 foot long piled pier – the first along the Lincolnshire coast. On August Bank holiday, opening day, 2,859 visitors paid 6d (2½p) for the privilege of promenading out over the sea; thereafter the price was 1d, attracting 37,000 visitors in its first five weeks. Cleethorpes Pier, with its elevated entrance from the cliff top gardens and a concert hall at the seaward end, was a successful attraction of the time and became the focus of the seafront and an important social meeting place.

The town's railway station was built in best Victorian building tradition, on a highly desirable northern promenade site. Excited passengers were brought directly to the promenade and immediately treated to views of the sea. The station changed little over the years, except for the addition of the clock that signalled the end of a day at the resort and the return home.

The MS&LR made substantial investments in Cleethorpes seafront over a number of years: the provision of swimming baths, refreshment rooms, three colonnades of shops, a restaurant and a photographic studio. Extensive gardens were laid out, complete with conservatory, and the Ross Castle folly was built. The works were reported to 'have entirely metamorphosed the frontage to the sea – commanding unqualified admiration'.

The *Bank Holidays Act* of 1871, cheap excursion trains from large population centres, organised works and Sunday school outings, all ensured the further development of the resorts through increased working class demand. Railway companies also began selling half price children's fares, propelling the family seaside holiday into existence.

Promenades, parks and gardens have come to characterise seaside resorts. But, during the late nineteenth and early twentieth centuries, the expense and lack of profit from these facilities meant the private sector could not keep them, and local government was once again required to intervene to subsidise amenities, for the benefit of both residents and visitors. The profitability of piers, bathing pools and some entertainment centres, such as theatres, also required subsidising due to the short seasonal nature of seaside tourism.

Social graces

The facilities of inland spas soon made an appearance, but, compared to the confines of the pump room, the open seashore was less restrictive and could accommodate an increasing range of people from different social backgrounds. The high prices charged for travel, accommodation and entertainment during the early fashionable years of the seaside ensured that the resorts remained exclusive and of a certain social tone and eloquence. Now, visitors were arriving from dissimilar, and often incompatible, backgrounds. They had different expectations of the seaside and holiday environment. Sophisticated segregation and social exclusion, that had been effective in the spas, was not acceptable on the open seashore areas, and there was competition for space on the foreshore, including the promenade, beach and seafront. The gradual mixing of the different social backgrounds of visitors began to cause problems of unacceptable behaviour for the respectable element and local people. At Cleethorpes, in 1872, it was reported that 'respectable locals [were] offended by people bathing without machines with hundreds looking on and seeming to enjoy the nude, rude and savage scene'.[2] Additionally, the increasing amount of drunkenness, brutal language and fights of the excursion trippers who spent much of their time in public houses affronted local people.

Cleethorpes was a socially unpretentious resort, adapting to accept a changing role for its wide variety of visitors. There was a shift of taste in entertainment – orchestras and balls gave way to brass bands; lectures and circulating libraries gave way to Pierrots, funfairs and amusements. There was no single focal point, and the adult social company of the pump room disintegrated into smaller units. The Victorian and Edwardian years were the 'Golden Years' of the seaside, with more and more facilities being developed to accommodate social changes – what had been a fishing village and resort for the genteel was now growing and changing into a popular working class resort.

Entertainment

The town's 1909 guide advertised: 'entertainment in amazing profusion', and a 'plentiful supply of canopied and hammock chairs provided by the Council, for visitors to bask in the beautiful sunshine in the most luxurious fashion possible'. During the era between the Wars, Cleethorpes was overwhelmed with working men and their families who streamed off the trains, past the clock tower, to the seafront.

From walking along the cliff top and strolling along the newly laid promenade, the variety of attractions increased rapidly. The pier, focus of the resort for many years, remained popular as a meeting place, for social gatherings and entertainment as well as being an extension to the promenade. Regular concerts attracted celebrities; there were dances, and the Cleethorpes Music Festival was held in the pier pavilion. The gardens, bathing pool and shops became increasingly overshadowed by the wealth of other attractions and amusements.

By the early 1950s, part of the appeal of Cleethorpes was its high cultural level that included a first class repertory company, operatic and dramatic performances, and its music festival attracting over 2,000 competitors. Now, the whole of the seafront was devoted to fun and pleasure with entertainment and all the fun of the fair. The beaches were extremely crowded, particularly at Bank Holiday weekends, where entertainment attracted hordes of people, with donkey rides, Punch and Judy shows, swing boats and the Big Wheel a familiar sight (Figures 3 and 4). The beach ventriloquist who drew

Figure 3. High Cliffe, Cleethorpes in 1861. *Grimsby Reference Library, North East Lincolnshire Council*

Figure 4. Promenade and Switchback. *Grimsby Reference Library, North East Lincolnshire Council*

large crowds to watch his performance had a pitch close to the pier; there were shrimp sellers, sand artists producing sand patterns, and children's competitions. The White Stars Concert Party performed on a portable stage on the beach entertaining crowds sat on rows of deckchairs. Levi Stephenson took boat trips in the *Cambridge Lass,* hailing: 'Come for a sail with old Levi, the man with the big nose'.

On the foreshore, Warwick Tower, with its spiral lift and revolving observation platform, gave panoramic views of the whole area, including Grimsby Docks. At Jessie Farquhar's tea-room, in the 'Grotto' in the pier gardens, one could sit on the terrace on fine sunny days overlooking the foreshore and partake of afternoon tea and home-made cakes. The red-jacketed figures of Hardy's Holiday Snaps photographers were prominent figures on the promenade, as they persuaded visitors to be 'snapped' for a personal souvenir of their trip to Cleethorpes.

Wonderland amusement park, with its Big Dipper, dodgems and carousel could entertain up to 20,000 people. Inside, there was the Ghost train, and skill tests such as darts, firing ranges and hoopla on side stalls. Arcades with slot machines, Fairy River and Jolly Boats, and Wall of Death motorcyclists provided entertainment, while towering overhead was the wooden rollercoaster (named Dip the Dips). Further south, the bathing pool, zoo and boating lake enticed visitors to walk or take a tram and see more of the growing resort.

So, on this north-east corner of Lincolnshire, most of the fun to be had was based around the seafront. In addition to the attractions and entertainment of the foreshore, the sea with its comings and goings – also provided an interest. Pleasure was gained from watching ships and boats entering and leaving the Humber Estuary, viewing Haile sand fort – the closest of the two defence forts built in 1915 – and inspecting the unusual items washed up on to the shore, such as ships, mines and even a whale. People liked to watch the constant ebb and flow of the tides over the sand, lapping round the cast iron pier legs and leaving pools of water where children fished for small fish and crabs.

The heyday of the British seaside holiday is but a memory, yet resorts remain attractive to a great many people who still visit and love the seaside holiday with its ingrained atmosphere (Figure 5). Regeneration officers may well have moved in to upgrade and modernise, but it still remains the seafront and foreshore that provides the interest and attractions most visitors come to see. The sea still holds a fascination for many, and the smell of the fresh sea air or a walk along the beach is still a pleasurable experience.

Figure 5. Beach and Pier. *Author's collection*

Figure 6. Cleethorpes' modern-day foreshore and gardens. *Author's collection*

Figure 7. Marine Embankment and Boating Lake. *Author's collection*

The borough of Cleethorpes has grown considerably over the years, both in size and population, but it is this small portion of seafront and foreshore that has made the town a holiday resort. Now, in the twenty-first century, those who still want to visit the town on warm summer days enjoy the foreshore; they sit in the gardens, watch the ships, walk along Marine Embankment, hire a boat on the boating lake or enjoy the thrills and spills of Pleasure Island (Figures 6 and 7).

Today, the foreshore is the scene for events, festivals, carnivals and galas that continue to attract people to Cleethorpes for that special day out. It is said in promotional literature: 'All the ingredients you expect of a traditional seaside resort are still alive in Cleethorpes. Four miles of safe sandy beaches, a superb events and festivals programme and a host of quality attractions.'

Here, people can feel free, forget worries and enjoy themselves.

Notes and References

1 Ekberg, Charles (1986). *The Book of Cleethorpes*. Barracuda Books, Buckingham.
2 Robinson, David (1981) *The Book of the Lincolnshire Seaside*. Barracuda Books, Buckingham.

Further Bibliography

Edward Drury (1981), *The Old Clee Story*.
J A R Pimlott (1944), *Englishman's Holiday - A Social History*. Faber & Faber, London.
John K Walton (1983), *The English Holiday Resort. A Social History 1750-1914*. Leicester University Press, St Martins Press New York.
John K Walton (2000), *The British Seaside. Holidays and resorts in the twentieth century*. Manchester University Press, Manchester.
Mike Walton and Joanne Mason (2000), *History of Seaside Tourism on the Yorkshire and Lincolnshire coasts*. Unpublished document produced for INTERREG IIC project: *Seaside Tourism in the North Sea Region*. University of Lincolnshire and Humberside.
D Pearce (1995), *Tourism Today: A Geographical Analysis*. Longman Scientific and Technical, Harlow.

9. LETTERS FROM A SEAMAN

by Jenny Walton

A BRICKLAYER, REPAIRING BOMB DAMAGE to a house at Main Street, Ulceby, discovered a rotting oilskin package in the false roof. On opening the package, the nonagenarian house owner found that it contained a number of very old letters – written by a seaman of His Majesty's Royal Navy (George III – 1738-1820). She passed the letters on to her daughter, a Scunthorpe resident. Claiming the letters brought her nothing but bad luck, the daughter hung them up outside her house, in the porch, hoping someone would steal them. But there they remained – until a descendant of that letter-writer, hearing of them via the local press in 1974, delightedly took them away. He was the late Ron Short (Figure 1), then living at South Killingholme, latterly at Immingham.

The letters were written by one George Neal, an ordinary man who went to sea and became an important cog in the wheel of

Figure 1. The late Ron Short, descendant of George Neal. *Mrs O Short*

Horatio Nelson's campaigns against Britain's enemies. Interestingly, George's first wife also had her part to play during the war years...

The seaman

George Neal was born on 16 February 1755, son of one William Neal. At the time of writing this chapter, it is not known where George was born, but we do know that a number of his family lived, for a time, in the Hull area and later, in the north of Lincolnshire. The year of George's birth was that when Samuel Johnson wrote: *A Dictionary of the English Language,* a volume that would be of use to only part of the country's population, in that era when much of the working population still could not read or write. George, however, certainly received a rudimentary literary education.

The mid-eighteenth century was a time of turmoil, especially for Britain and its European enemies – France, in particular. Russia, Austria, and Prussia were the other main European powers, whilst Spain, although not as strong, was in possession of a reasonably proficient navy. Yet, as good as Spain's ocean-going forces were, superiority of the seas belonged to Britain, followed a close second by the French Navy.

Any intermittent peaceful periods were shortlived and a luxury that could not be relied upon to last.

A year after George's birth, the Seven Years War began, and Britain, allied with Prussia and Portugal, sent her men out to fight, on land and sea, the enemy: France, Austria, Russia, Sweden and Saxony. Perhaps it was growing up in this atmosphere that led George Neal to decide upon a career at sea, but, fortunately for posterity, while he served in the Navy he wrote to his family back home. Forty-one of these letters have survived, covering the period from 1776 until 1843. In varying stages of quality and legibility, their ink faded brown and faint on papers that, because they were folded over and over before being sealed and tied for posting, are not always in whole pieces. But date stamps can still be read on most of them, and there is evidence of wax seals – indeed, on some, the actual seal, itself, still exists.

George's writing skills were good, although punctuation is almost non-existent and spelling in the earlier letters is, at times phonetical – showing only too clearly his northern background; but, over the years, his grasp of spelling improves. The letter thought to be the oldest has only the date of 28 December, but, unusually for him, no year. Nor does it have a postmark, so it is the only one that cannot be dated exactly. Written from Portsmouth, George sent it to his father, William Neal, addressed thus:

> *Mr*
> *William Neal to Be Left*
> *at Mr John Coannells[1] in*
> *Black fryer Gate alleys*
> *Hull*
> *yorkshir*

Ever the respectful son, George wrote:

> *Honered father this With my Love and Duty to you hopin these Lines Will find you in Good health as I am at Present I Blefs God for it I Receaved your Letter and Was sorey to here of my Brother Being ill and I rote an ancer But as not Receaved an nother Which makes me think you Did not Receave the Letter I Rote But I hope you Will Git this I still Remain in the same sitteuation and Expects to Remain as such if nothing happens to the contrary I Shall Be Glad of an ancer as soun as this comes to hand so no more at Present from your Dutyfull and Well Wishing sun, My love to all frends. George Neal and I Wish you all a hapy New year.*

On 26 November 1776, writing from aboard *The Princess of Medlea*,[2] he tells his father: *this coms with my cind love to you* and that:

> *we are now Lying upon the Neither Bank ny Porchmouth* [Portsmouth] *we have been hear this fortneet wating for Sum Ships that are goin in our fleet we have had a Strong gail of wind we was forst to Strik our yards* [next word cannot be read] *Topmasts but we Rid it out with* [word cannot be read] *anchor and a hundered Sail more of Marchant men* [Merchant seamen] *with us the wind is comd to the Nored So we Expect to Sail verey soun to morrow is the Day apointed for us to Sail if wind and Weather permits so this is the this the Last oppertunety I Shall have of Wrighting at this place...*

Continuing with the information that he has often been ashore on *Ile of Wite it is a fine plentiful place so we can get any thing we want*, and that he has once been to *Porchmouth*, he comments that he and the crew are able to:

> *go any wear with out being Melested* [molested] *with the Presf gang they are Presfing all they can com at out of the whomard* [homeward] *Bound Ships I am afraid they are Presin hot at hull it*

*was a great providence that I did not come to hull for I had a great
thouat of it wonce... Give my cind love to my Sister and Brothers and
all well wishing friends I am a little uneasey as have not heard from
you I rote at london to Misis Coaney*[3] *and desired her to send me an
ancer how you all was... I have had none yet I whope you recived my
monthly pay and I whope you have paid Willy Norton as I rote in one
letter before...*

George instructs his father to pay off various debts that he *hows*
[owes] and *houd* [owed], such as that of ten hats costing ten shillings
...then I Shall be all clear in the world...

The year he wrote this letter, Britain had recruited 29,000 Hessian
mercenaries for the American War of Independence; for the first
time, a motion had been put before the Commons to abolish slavery
in Britain and the British colonies; Barrow-upon-Humber's John
Harrison, watchmaker and inventor of the chronometer, died (24
March), and John Constable, the artist was born (11 June). So, too,
did American Congress draw up and pass the Declaration of
Independence (4 July) and, a week later, Captain Cook sailed from
Plymouth in the *Resolution*, accompanied by the *Discovery*, on his
third and last expedition. All distant news to George, no doubt.

In his next letter from *Princess of Medlea*, dated 24 June 1779,
George tells his father that the vessel is lying at Spit Head as a Guard
Ship. He is happy that he and four other crew members are the
Admiral's

*Barg men and he allways stays on shore and we the same so I am in
hopes from going to sea this sumer I am verey hapy at Present and
have nothing to make me uneasy... I am belonging to Sir Thomas Shy
Which is Chief commander at spitt head I am free from the Daingers
of the seas and Like wise the Ennemys...*

With the request that he be sent his

*cote and wast cote and Paed Jakit and any of my close that you think
Will not Be any use to your self... it may Be along time Before I can
com to them...*

By 8 September 1783, he is living at Chatham, near the dockyard on
the River Medway. It would appear his father has died, as the letters
are now being sent to his sister Mary and her husband, Thomas
Short, also in Hull. George requests they send him various items,
including a bedstead and a pair of bouts [boots] because

the Bouts that they make hear is not Worth half the money that they

> *Charge for them if you Git me a pare Let them Be Black in the Grane*
> *and Prity Lite With a Good Long tops You can git them mad*[e] *and*
> *Send them...*

One theme that runs consistently through all George's letters is that
he is not receiving replies to the missives he sends them. Coming over
almost as a complaint each time, he then usually notes that perhaps
they have not actually received his letters. Understandably, when you
think of mail packages having to travel from ship to shore and across
a country of unrest.

By 1785, we find that, having given the latest news about himself
and his state of health and wellbeing, his religion has become very
important to him. A chapel man, probably Methodist according to a
later letter, he deems it his duty to sermonise in great depth and
length, instructing his sister, Mary, and her husband:

> *I am afraid you are Still Living in neglect of your Preshous and*
> *Enmortal Souls Which are of moore valleu then the hole World... But*
> *I have to Bemone and Simpithise concarning you being in so Dark*
> *a place you have But verey little Light of the Blessed Word of God to*
> *What We have at Chatham... I could say a Great Deal moore but my*
> *paper his Expendod So I conclude With my sinceare Wishes to the*
> *Wellfair of your souls and Bodyes may the Lord Blefs you all Amen*

For the rest of his life, George gives plenty of paper room to his
sermons, sometimes two or three pages of them with little personal
news, and, although it is obvious he does receive replies, one can only
wonder if his dear relatives would have preferred less heavy reading
in order to encourage their more ready response.

Meanwhile, France endured a Revolution, wherein the common
people rose up against its Royal family and all those wealthy
aristocrats who had steadfastly maintained a clear line between the
'haves' and the 'have nots'. Beginning in 1789, it lasted until 1799
when Napoleon took over the government. The result of the
revolution left that country's wealth somewhat more evenly
distributed – for a time.

On 21 April 1791, via a letter to his sister and brother-in-law now
living at: *Imingham* near *Caster*, we learn that he is in *Exzpectacion of*
Being made Gunner of a man of Ware. An immensely responsible
position, a gunner was only appointed after passing an examination
and serving one year as a petty officer. Now a warrant officer, he
would be the only gunner on board and would now have a cabin of
his own, instead of sharing the common below-deck accommodation

where the ordinary seamen lived. He was mainly responsible for maintenance of guns and armament, rather than the actual firing, and was in charge of the gun room and of the boys who lodged there. This latter role was taken from many gunners by the nineteenth century. This letter is the only one which he signs from both himself and his wife, Elizabeth.

Less than five months after the French Republic (Convention) declares war on Britain and Holland and three months after it has declared war on Spain, on 10 June 1793 George writes:

> *I have Left my old Cittiuation... Left Chatham and the yatch and am gunner of His Majestys Sloop of War the* Scourge *Which I think I hinted to you in sum of my Letters that I was in Expecttacion of a Gunners Warrant sum time Back so now I have no Setled Place of a Boad Sum times I am in one port and sum in another For the Present my Sittiuaction is verey Disagreable... We Have Had a verey sevear Ingagement With a French Privatear and have took her and a French merchant ship and Brought them safe into port so the Lord still Continues His Goodnefs to me a unworthy Worm in Preserving me from the Dangers of the seas and the Dangers of the Ennemy I hope I shall yet see you aGain...*

On 19 December 1793, Toulon, an important Mediterranean French naval base, fell to the British, who burnt its stores and ships. By 19 July 1796, when George writes from the renowned 74-gun *Goliath* where it is anchored off Toulon, Horatio Nelson and Napoleon Bonaparte have arisen as the starring adversaries, representing Britain and France respectively, in the continuing battle for supremacy between the two countries.

George has to send his letter home via another ship leaving for England:

> *...have verey Little timme to Write I have the happenefs to a Quaint you my Wife and I oft Injoy a verey Good state of health. we are Watching the French Fleet of Toulon Expect to have a verey seveare Battle with them verey Shortly if it Please god to spare me it tis not Likely We shall Retorn to England till the Ware is Ended... I Did not Expect my Wife at that time Would go to sea with me but as our Destination Were alterd she came to a Determination to go With me Seperations being Verey uncomfortable...* (Figure 2)

This letter was, once again, addressed to his sister, Mary, and her husband, at *Emingham, Near Castor, Lincolnshire.*

This mention of his wife accompanying him to sea is indicative of

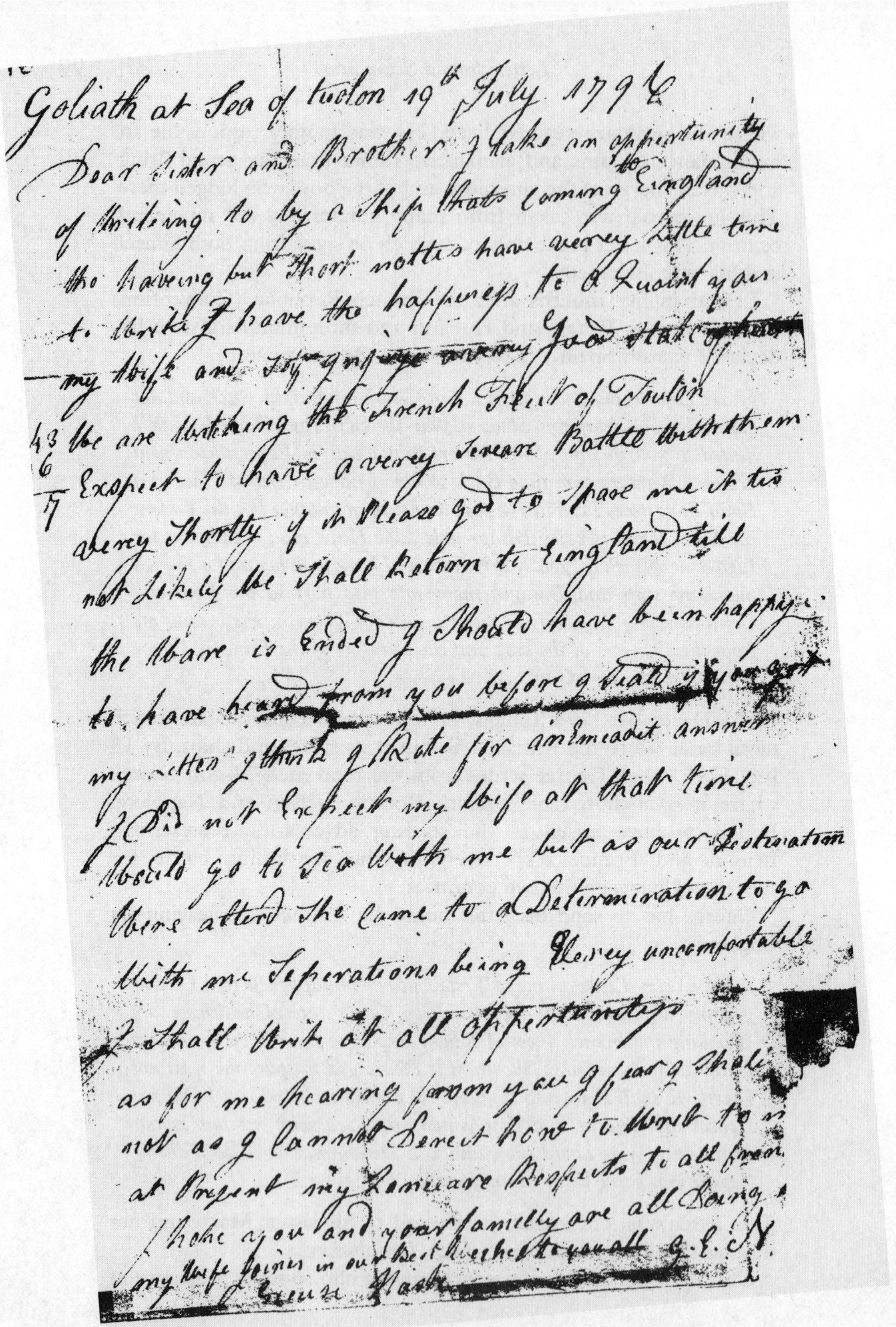

Goliath at Sea of tuelon 19th July 1796

Dear Sister and Brother I take an opportunity of Writing to by a Ship thats coming to England the haveing but short notice have veorey little time to Write I have the happeneps to Aquaint you my Wife and Self ynjoying very Good state of heart We are Wathing the French Fleet of Toulon Exspect to have a verey Severe Battle with them veery Shortly if it Please God to Spare me it tis not likely We Shall Return to England till the Ware is Ended I Should have been happey to have heard from you before I Sail if you get my Letter I think I Wate for an Emeadit answer I Did not Exspeck my Wife at that time Should go to Sea With me but as our Destenation Were alterd She came to a Determination to go With me Seperations being Veery uncomfortable I Shall Writ at all oppertunites as for me hearing from you I fear I Shall not as I cannot derect how to Writ to m at Present my Loveare Respects to all from I hope you and your familey are all Doing my Wife Joines in our Best Weehesto youall G. & N

Figure 2. Part of a letter written by George Neal, dated 19 July 1796.
Mrs O Short

the regularity with which women – that is, usually wives of officers or petty officers – accompanied their men, even during times of battle. They had their own roles on board ship, mainly looking after the wounded and sick.

In 1795, Holland joined with France against Britain and, on 8 October, the next year, Spain also declared war on Britain. The last invasion of Britain failed when 1,400 French troops, under the command of the Irish-American general Tate, landed in Dyfed on 12 February 1797, only to surrender to British soldiers. Two days later, the Battle of Cape St Vincent took place on the River Tagus, near Lisbon in Portugal, and Britain, led by Nelson, defeated the Spanish fleet. We know that the *Goliath* was part of that fleet, but the first correspondence we have from George Neal after that great battle was dated 16 December that same year. He makes no direct reference to that particular battle.

However, he does write that he has been at sea for eight months aboard the *Goliath*, with expectation of another eight to ten months sailing ahead of him. He also expresses weariness at being away from his native country, and, although his wife is still with him, they are both *exposed to the Dangers of the Seas and of being snached awy by Death before we Reach England again*. For this reason, he decides it would be prudent to advise his relatives that if he and his wife do not survive, they should contact the Navy Agent at 13 Clements Inn, Strand, London. Another sheet within the package contains his will. Handwritten, somewhat rambling and informal, it reveals that George's kin would be able to collect between £250 and £260 in cash, wages and prize money[4] included, should he and his wife die whilst at sea. There is also some property. He continues:

> *...if my sister is or should be Dead her eldest son I believe Will be the proper are* [heir] *and the only Percon that can Recover what belongs to me after both our Deaths, but We Will Leave this Dark sean* [scene] *and I hope to se Each other again in this Life if it should please God so...*

Seamen scribbling out hastily composed wills and possible last letters to their families was a normal activity in those final minutes before battle commenced. In such times, it was not surprising that so many of them peppered their correspondence with references to God, hoping for his blessing and watchful eye over their safety. The strain of their long sojourns at sea, the dangers they constantly faced in battle and whilst patrolling foreign waters, all added to the pressure they were under – from the youngest lad to the captain.

Mr and Mrs George Neal survive, however. On 4 February 1799

George writes to his sister and brother-in-law again, from the *Goliath*, on the Island of Malta:

> *Aftther a long time silence... opportunity offers to Let you hear from me by Favour of an officer coming to England. I write in Hast to a Quaint you that I and my wife are still in being and thanks be to the almighty... you no doubth have heard of the Dreadfull Infringment we had with the French Fleet the first of August 1798 when we took and destroyed the Greattist Part of there Fleet. since that we have Been in Great hopes of coming home to England as our Ship is verey much ought of order by being constantly at sea and by being much dammaged in the matter with the Spanish and French Fleets...*

The 'dreadful infringement' of which he speaks is, of course, the famous *Battle of the Nile*. Nelson, now a Rear Admiral, had been pursuing the French fleet since 1798, after Britain had learned Napoleon's large naval expedition was planning an invasion of Egypt in order to threaten British possession of India and to restrict its trade routes. The French fleet, under Admiral François-Paul Brueys d'Aigailliers, consisting of thirteen ships of the line and four frigates, however, had been managing to keep one step ahead of the British convoy of fourteen vessels, until they were finally sighted, anchored in the bay of Aboukir (Abu Qir) near Alexandria, Egypt. It was almost night; the French were in a strong defensive line in the sandy bay, and they were protected on the one side by a shore battery, yet Nelson ordered an immediate attack.

Captain Thomas Foley of the *Goliath*, seeing a gap in the enemy defence, took what was undoubtedly a risky, yet effective, manoeuvre, and sailed around the head of the French fleet on the landward side to take up position behind their lines. He was followed by three other British vessels. Although one went aground, they caused tremendous damage to the startled French, while Nelson led the rest of the fleet to create a nutcracker effect. As good as the French were, they inevitably suffered defeat. Once their flagship was hit and had caught fire, it blew up and the battle was as good as over. Admiral Brueys was killed, and only two of the French fleet's battleships and two frigates escaped.

Our man, George Neal, was aboard the *Goliath*, once again in the midst of a fierce battle. But here, a fascinating point must be noted. It was his wife, Elizabeth, who went down in historical accounts. Twenty-four years after this battle a small book, written by one John Nichol recollecting his time as a naval man, was published. He was a signal midshipman on the *Goliath* and wrote:

> *I was much indebted to the Gunner's wife who* [during the battle] *gave her husband and me a drink of wine every now and then...*

This account has since been used in many historical works.

The war went on, and in January of 1799, a month before George's last mentioned letter home, Prime Minister William Pitt the Younger introduced a tax of two shillings (10p) in the pound on incomes over £200, to raise money for the war effort.

George's next missive, informing everyone back home that he had arrived safely back in England, was sent later that year, on 12 November, whilst the *Goliath* was at the naval base of Spithead.

> *and thanks be to Almighty God I and my wife are Both in a tollerable Good state of Health I have Rote Several Letters to you Since I Left England Weather you have Receaved any or not I at Present Cannot tell... my Wife and Self have Esxpearenced a Great Deal of Truble since we Left England – had sum verey narrow Escapes for our Lives But thanks be to Gracious God we are Spaird as monuments of his mercy and I hope we Shall be Enabled to tell of his Goodnefs in the Land of the Living we Expect our Ship will be Shortly up into Portsmouth harber for she wants a Great deal of Repairs...*

There is obviously some shore leave as he occasionally writes from his home addresses in and around Portsea, but, according to his letter of 24 October 1803, regardless of his wish to leave the sea, 48 year-old George is still serving on the *Goliath* in HM's navy, and, sadly, his wife had died at home the previous June after a very long illness.

> *I under stand her disorder Lay so much in her head that she Lost her Sences for agreat Lenth of time...*

He is now showing further signs of dissatisfaction at having to remain in the Navy, claiming to be wearey of the life. He continues:

> *...if you are still Liviing you must feel the afects of old age Which is the case with me I have indured a Great deal of hardships...*

Two months later, he writes again from Portsmouth harbour with the information he is now serving aboard the *Guilford* [sic]. He describes her as

Laying in a state of what they call ordinery that is a ship not Likely to go to Sea I was not very Well in Health and Grew [quite?] Wiary of the sea so I Expect to stay at home at least this Winter perhaps Longer Except I Get a Larger ship... but I hope now to have a Little Rest...

Before instructing them to seek their salvation, and to be aware of the goodness of God, he talks of England making preparations for an invasion, thus not allowing him to get out of Portsmouth and make the journey to Lincolnshire to see them all.

His next ship appears to be the *Kent,* another 74-gun vessel, from which he writes in September, 1805 whilst they are on the River Medway, and February, 1806 when at Plymouth.

O am again abought to Incounter With the Perrels & Daingers of the Seas Which I have oftton dun before, & the Lord hath in Great Mercy Spard me & preserved me... I Expect I am Going to the Mideteraenen once more I Expect to Sail in a day or two From plymouth in Hs Majestyes Ship Kent *captain garrett and Admiral Thornbourh having his Flag on board...*

He goes on to tell them, delightedly, that he has married:

a widdow at Portsea aimiable in Person & carractter... I Left her in Great Destrefs and Greife of mind on the account of our Sepperation Indeed I Feel it verey trying my Self for We are Exceeding That we call in common fond of Each other... I have well on to five years Longer to Serve before I am Intitld to Supperanuation or be Quiet Free from the Servise then if it Please the Lord to Spare me till that time I can Git free from serving in any Ship...

George's letter of 2 March 1807 is written in response to the news his sister, Mary, has died. He urges his brother-in-law, Thomas to allow God to support and help him during this bad time. Over the years, he continues to correspond with Thomas, as does his new wife when George, himself, is at sea.

Surprisingly, we find he is still a naval man as he nears his sixty-second birthday. Still writing to his brother-in-law, now living at Thomas Rutland's, Bricklayer, Kirmington, he says on 14 November 1816:

I have Been Expecting for three years Back to Get Superanuated that is Get Cleare of the kings Service but I Still Remain as I ws only I have no Ship the Ship I had hase Been Broke up more than 12 months But I hope to get another verey Shortly or be Superanuated of the Latter I Can Go where I Please and it Please the Lord to spare

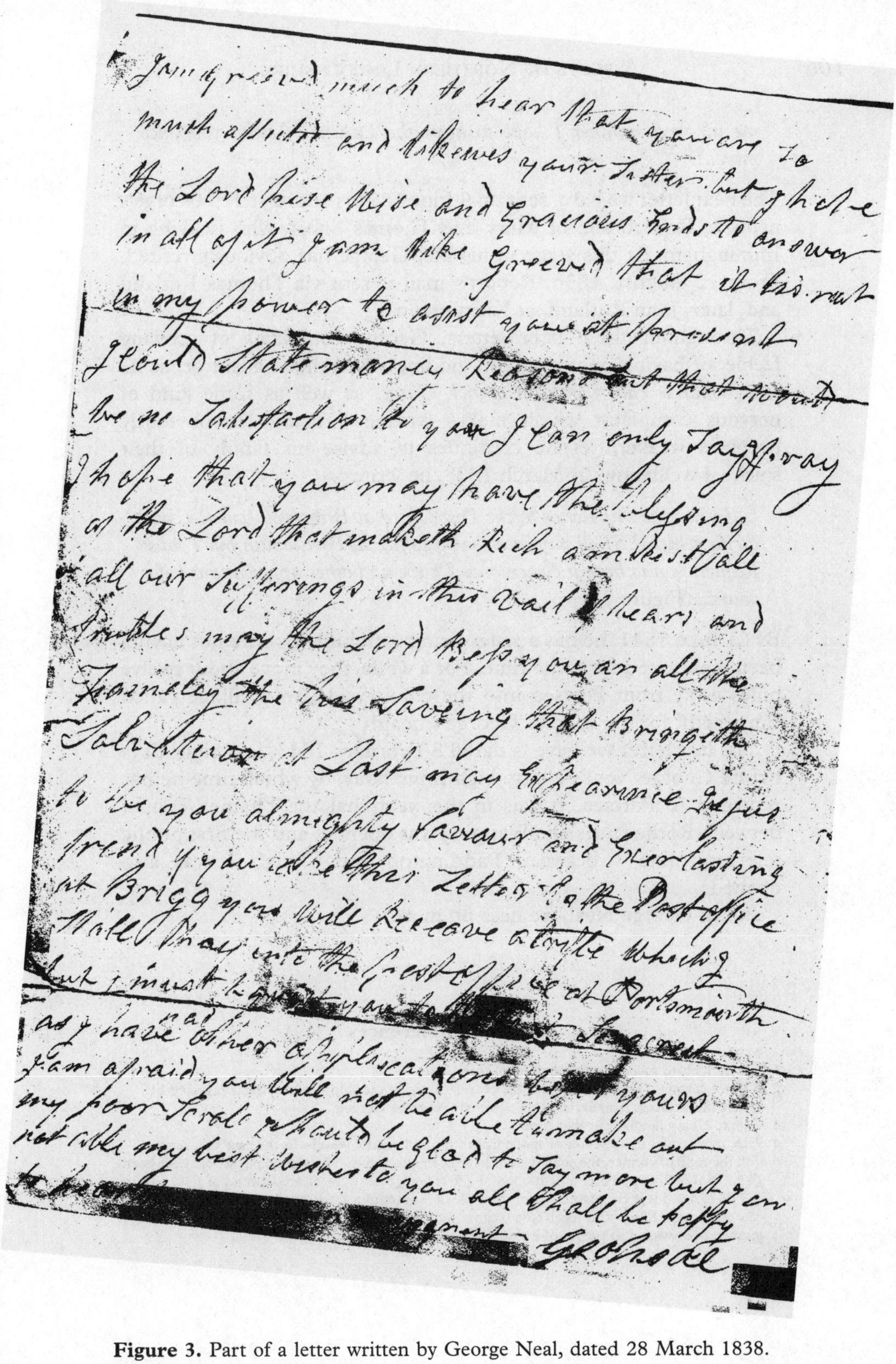
I am greived much to hear that you are
much afflicted and likewes your sister to
the Lord hise wise and Gracious hands to answer but I hope
in all of it I am like Greived that it is not
in my power to asist you at present
I could state many Reasons but that would
be no satisfaction to you I can only say pray
I hope that you may have the blessing
of the Lord that maketh Rich and adds to all
all our sufferings in this vail of tears and
troubles may the Lord bless you an all the
family the tru saving that bringeth
Salvation at last may the ... Jesus
to be you almighty saviour and Everlasting
friend if you direct their Letter to the Post office
at Brigg you will Receive it by the ...
Mail ... into the Post office
but I must ... at Portsmouth
as I have other applications ... yours
I am afraid you will not be able to make out
my poor scrawl I should be glad to say more but I am
not able my best wishes to you all shall be happy
to hear ...
GeoNeal

Figure 3. Part of a letter written by George Neal, dated 28 March 1838.
Mrs O Short

me till next summer I hope to have the Pleasur of seing you once more...

The next letter we have, sent on 9 June 1824 is addressed to George's nephew, Robert, son of Mary and Thomas Short, who is living in Immingham. At this stage in his life, George has obviously retired. From 12 August, 1836, Robert's mail is sent via Thomas Rutland and, later, John Rutland, at Kirmington.

Throughout these later letters, George complains of growing feeble, of having poor eyesight, giddiness and rheumatism or, as he says: *what is cald the Rumematick Gaute,* as well as some kind of nervous complaint which makes writing difficult. He obviously becomes weaker, yet he continues to advise his family of their spiritual wellbeing. In March 1838, he writes:

> *...if you take this Letter to the Post Office at Brigg you will Receave atrifle which I Shall pay into the postoffice at Portsmouth but I must Request you to keep it Seacrert as I have had other applycations befor yours...*(Figure 3).

By 21 June 1841, he has a sister living with him, his wife not having been mentioned for some time. For a while, they move about twelve miles away from Portsea into the countryside, to a village called Emsworth, for the sake of George's health.

The last letter we have is dated 8 February 1843, just eight days before George Neal's eighty-eighth birthday, by which time he has returned to Portsea. It was in this year that the Thames Tunnel between Rotherhithe and Wapping was opened, and the first public telegraph line – between Paddington and Slough – was also opened.

But of George Neal, we hear no more.

Notes and References

1 It is difficult to make out the spelling of this name.
2 It is not certain if George Neal has the correct name of the ship – it has been suggested he means the Princess Amelia, but this point has yet to be verified.
3 George Neal's landlady at that time.
4 Prize money was the division of spoils from captured enemy vessels. In the case of a seaman with the rank of gunner, the share would have been one-eighth. His annual pay would have been £83. 12s. (£83. 60p). After a deduction of £5 0s 6d (£5. 2½), he cleared a total of £77. 11s.6d (£77.57½) – this is compared to, for example, a captain of a 1st Rate ship (the 74-gun *Goliath* was classed 1st Rate) who received a clear annual pay of £721. 16s 2d (£721. 81p); and a gunner, boatswain and purser of a sloop who cleared £48. 13s 6d (£48. 67½).

Acknowledgements

The late Ron Short, and his wife, Olga, of Immingham.
Immingham Library, especially Brenda, Margaret and Susan (for whom nothing is too much trouble).
The National Maritime Museum.
Alan King, Historical Collections Librarian, Portsmouth City Library.
Peter Goodwin, Keeper and Curator, HMS *Victory*, HM Naval Base, Portsmouth.
Matthew Sheldon, Curator of Manuscripts, Royal Naval Museum, Portsmouth.

Bibliography

The Wooden World by N A M Rodger
Britannia Rules by C Northcote Parkinson
The Napoleonic Wars by Gunther Rothenberg
The Battle of the Nile by Oliver Warner
Nelson's Navy by Brian Lavers

10. Some aspects of a Pre-Enclosure Farm in Barrow-upon-Humber

by Neil R Wilkyn

THERE IS, IN THE LINCOLNSHIRE Archives Office, a farming memorandum book and diary belonging to the Wilkin[1] family, who were prominent in Barrow-upon-Humber from the sixteenth to the nineteenth centuries. It is a small exercise book containing the entries written by two brothers, Samuel and Laurence Wilkin, between 1714 and 1741. As Samuel Wilkin died in 1733, the majority of the entries were written by Laurence Wilkin. Only a few are personal, most of them being concerned with the different aspects of their farming activities within the open fields of the village.

The Family

The Wilkin family had been resident in Barrow since at least the 1530s. Parish registers tell us that John Wilkyn was born there around 1536. He married Isabel Sergeant, a member of another of Barrow's illustrious families, in 1568. It was one of their many grandsons, Thomas Wilkyn, born in 1619, who was founder of the branch to which Laurence and Samuel belonged. In the sixteenth, century the Wilkins had been substantial farmers with fine possessions and a good house.

John was buried in 1596, as befitted a man of some status, within the nave of the parish church 'as nere the alter and whereas I used to sett as convenyenthe maie be...'.[2] He left land and property in both Barrow and Hessle (just across the Humber) and a good sum of money to his family and friends. Over the following generations, the arrival of many sons and the need to divide land between them reduced the family fortunes somewhat, but by the beginning of the eighteenth century, Laurence and Samuel were again building up a considerable farm. Their father, George Wilkin, had married Ann Uppleby, a member of a family who had influence in the village as lords of one of the manors and who eventually built Barrow Hall.

The Parish

Barrow-upon-Humber is a parish of around 5,000 acres situated where the Lincolnshire Wolds slope down to the southern bank of the

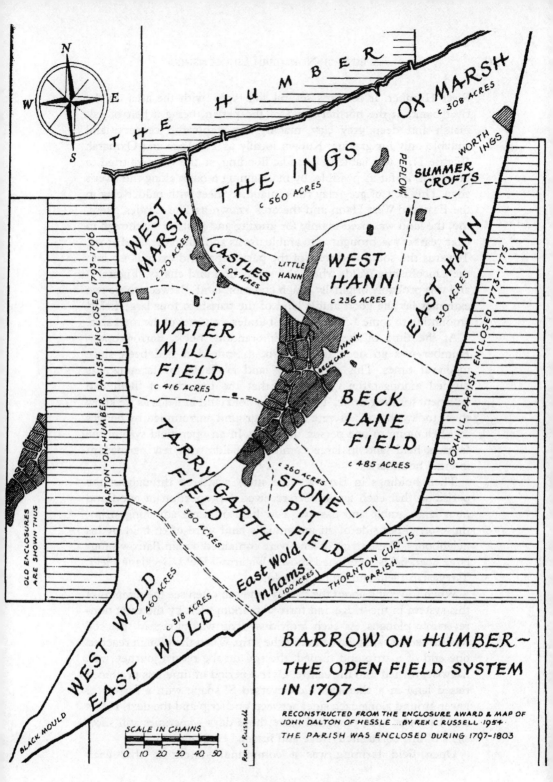

Figure 1. Pre-Enclosure map of Barrow-upon-Furness. *By courtesy of Rex C Russell.*

River Humber. It contains several soil types, with the area on the river bank, at the northern end of the parish, being a belt of salt marsh and deep grey clay, making the eighteenth century land suitable only for grazing. Known locally as The Ings and Oxmarsh (Figure 1), it was liable to periodic flooding, so the villagers tried to protect it, as far as possible, by maintaining a bank along the river's edge. This belt of grey clay runs inland to meet with redder clay in the East and West Hann and the area known as The Castles. Here, too, the land was used mainly for grazing and pasture – although in later years it was brought in to arable use as and when the need arose. Towards the south and west of the parish the land extends up into the Lincolnshire Wolds where the soil is thin and chalky (Figure 1) and was probably originally rough common land. Between these two extremes lay the good arable land of the parish in four large fields, amounting to some 1,520 acres, just under a quarter of the total area.

At the time of the Wilkin memorandum book, Barrow-upon-Humber was an open field parish, as indeed it had been since medieval times. This meant that land available for farming was divided amongst the villagers so that the majority of them had sufficient for their needs. They did not hold land in fields as we know them today, that is, discrete areas of ground surrounded by hedges and belonging to one person or family. In an open field system the farmers held land in large communal fields with few permanent internal boundaries.

Their holdings in Barrow were strips scattered throughout the parish so that each landholder received a proportion of good and poor land, arable and pasture. Few held multiple adjoining strips, those on either side of an individual's land were often held by his neighbours. These strips of land were contained within Barrow's four large open fields mentioned above – Watermill Field, Becklane Field, Tarrygarth Field and Stonepit Field.

When travelling about the county, one can often see the remains of this system in the 'ridge and furrow' markings left by the early non-reversible ploughs. As each individual strip was ploughed, the soil was turned towards the centre of the strip. When the plough reached one end of a strip and turned, the soil on the return journey was, likewise, turned into the centre. Over a period of time this produced raised land in a characteristic 'reversed S' shape with a furrow of lower ground along each side, between one strip and the next. Fields that have not been ploughed since those days sometimes still show signs of this corrugated 'ridge and furrow' even now.

Open field farming was a communal system in that each

landholder had to grow and harvest a similar crop to his neighbour in any one block of strips. It would have been chaotic had each farmer decided to grow his own crops on his own strips without consultation with the adjacent strip holders. The whole system was run by the village or manor court that met regularly to decide what should be grown where and by whom. This was no haphazard affair, but well regulated with written rules that had to be obeyed upon pain of punishment or penalties. These rules formed the original 'bye-laws' of the village and can still be read in the Barrow Town Book that dates from 1553.[3]

The Farm – Sheep

How did the Wilkin farm fit into this landscape? Laurence Wilkin had a mixed farm, as indeed did most farmers of this period. The days of the specialised farmer were still well into the future so Laurence had both crops and livestock. He grew wheat, barley and pulses in approximately equal amounts of some fifty acres each on his scattered holdings within the open fields, but perhaps his main interest lay in the rearing of sheep. Wool production in Lincolnshire had long been renowned, and during the eighteenth century the county was just entering the phase of long wool production for the worsted industries of Norfolk and Yorkshire, where water-powered mills were to form the early stirrings of the Industrial Revolution.

The vast majority of sheep reared in the eighteenth century were done so for their wool rather than for their meat, the production of which was very much of secondary importance. Sheep flesh was hardly ever eaten as lamb, and the prices of mutton in the early eighteenth century show the disdain with which it was regarded. Mutton was generally priced as low as tuppence or tuppence-halfpenny (1p) per pound. In Barrow and the surrounding villages, the average flock of sheep held by individuals was twenty, whereas Laurence Wilkin had around 200 animals. They were grazed on the common land of Barrow and on the stubble of the open fields after harvest according to the rules laid down in the Town Book. The arable fields were generally opened to sheep after 1 November and the meadow lands from 11 November to 2 March. The entries in the diary relating to Laurence Wilkin's sheep cover the years 1733 to 1741 and give us a valuable insight into how he managed his flock.

In 1733 Laurence took over the farm from his brother Samuel who had just died and the entry for this year shows him buying sheep in from outside the locality, probably to build up his flock with fresh blood. He attended the well-known sheep market at Caistor where he bought 20 hogs at just over seven shillings (35p) each and a further 10 hogs at 7s 2d each (36p). A hog is a sheep after it has formed two adult teeth – that is, when it is about one year old. Laurence also visited Kirton (in Lindsey) and bought 30 hogs at 6s 8d (33p) each and ten shearing sheep at 4s 2d (21p) each. He spent a total of £25 3s 6d (£25 17½p) on building up his flock in 1733 – a considerable sum.

Every year, the flock was counted and marked, usually in mid April. This way he would know the state his sheep were in after the winter ravages and after their lambs had been born. The animals were

Figure 2. A shepherd and his flock. *From Richard Bradley's 'Gentleman's and Farmer's Guide'.*

counted as adult sheep and lambs, and the number of dead animals was recorded. In 1736, it was noted that two lambs had been 'worred'(sic), presumably attacked by either dogs or foxes. Such occurrences can't have been uncommon amongst sheep in open fields protected only by temporary hurdles and the perhaps less-than-watchful eye of the shepherd.

Throughout the years 1733 to 1739 the flock remained fairly constant at around two hundred, but in 1740 disaster struck. In 1739 Laurence Wilkin had owned 266 animals, yet on 11 June 1740, at clipping time, there were only 128 counted. Similarly, in 1741, there were just 115 sheep in the flock. Research has shown that in 1740 there was an outbreak of sheep rot in the village which decimated many flocks and it was probably this that reduced Laurence's sheep numbers by over half. Sheep rot of this kind was almost certainly caused by the liver fluke parasite, a form of flat worm that lives in, and eventually destroys, a sheep's liver. It was common on wet grazing land, living in the water snail as part of its life cycle and being picked up whilst the sheep were grazing (Figure 2).

The grazing land of Barrow was predominantly situated in the lower, marshy areas of the parish in the Ings and Westmarsh – land that was prone to periodic flooding from the River Humber. Had the farmers' individual flocks been feeding in enclosed fields the disease would have been easier to control, but grazing as they did in the large open common ground together with other flocks, it was almost impossible to prevent the parasite spreading. As the diary entries ceased in 1741 we do not know whether Laurence ever managed to restore his flock to its former numbers.

The diary also tells us how much wool was clipped each year and to whom it was sold. Figures show that each sheep, on average, yielded between two and three pounds of wool, poor return, indeed, by today's standards. We also know that in his most successful year, 1739, Laurence received £21 6s (£21 30p) for his flock's wool, whilst in 1735 it had been only £7 18s (£7 90p). This is mainly because the fluctuating price for raw wool was low in the early 1730s, picking up after 1738. After the disaster of 1740, Laurence only managed £9 9s (£9 45p) for two years' wool combined.

How did Laurence Wilkin dispose of his wool? In the eighteenth century, most wool grown by small farmers was sold to the woollen industries of Norfolk, or Halifax and Wakefield in the West Riding of Yorkshire, where water-power drove the mills of the burgeoning textile industry. The clipped fleeces were taken by wool-jobbers or middlemen who travelled around the area collecting the wool from the farmers. Laurence sold his fleeces to several middlemen over the years, Messrs Stainfield and Stevenson being the main ones. Surname research has shown that Stainfield and Stevenson are common names in and around Wakefield, so it may be that Laurence's wool was going to the Yorkshire market.

Having struck a deal with the buyer, the farmer would have his wool packed and sealed ready for collection. Payment was often in the form of credit, which would be paid on the following Lady Day (25 March), in time to be used to buy the next season's stock. The flock was often deliberately reduced in winter to help conserve foodstuff, a vital consideration in the time before turnips and other root crops were to be made available for winter feeding of animals.

Before leaving the sheep and moving on to the crops that were being grown in eighteenth century Barrow-upon-Humber, there is a final element to be considered. It is the one thing that links livestock and crops together, and was crucial in the successful running of a farm in the time before synthetic fertilisers: manure. Early entries in the memorandum book are a statement of the manuring schedules that Samuel Wilkin and, later, Laurence Wilkin, employed to help enrich their land holdings. They consist of a description of the land onto which manure was spread each year from 1719 to 1734. It was said in the 1770s that 'an hundred sheep will, in one summer, enrich eight acres of ground which will continue its fertility six years'.[4]

Manuring was carried out by applying sheep droppings to the land, systematically – acre by acre. This was done by folding the flock overnight on land after the crops had been harvested, allowing the farmer to ensure his land in its scattered strips all received sufficient manure in any one season. That is why the schedules were so important. In the true spirit of communal farming, landholders often pooled their resources, as evidenced in the diary of Laurence Wilkin who shared his sheep manure with other farmers in the village, the whole process being regulated by a shepherd hired for the business.

In the large open fields it was no easy matter to ensure even distribution of this vital resource. The schedules were very detailed, making use of local landmarks and other landscape features such as trees, bushes, boundary markers and contours. Some of these features are still recognisable today, although many were lost when the parish was enclosed at the end of the eighteenth century. Great reliance was put on the knowledge and familiarity of their parish that local landholders had gleaned over many generations. Topographical details were of paramount importance in the large and essentially featureless expanses of the open fields.

Crops

In common with the other farmers in Barrow, Laurence Wilkin grew wheat, barley and pulses in approximately equal measure. The period covered by the memorandum book was before the widespread use of such specialist crops as clover, sainfoin or turnips which, although in limited use elsewhere in order to improve fertility, or provide winter fodder, talk of which had yet to reach the ears of Barrow's farmers. Having land in strips within an open field somewhat limited the variety of crops that could be grown and certainly precluded much in the way of experimentation. The only means of trying anything new was if one had an isolated enclosed piece of ground out in the parish and, although Laurence Wilkin did have such an enclosure, there is no evidence in the book that he was experimenting with innovative crops.

In 1734, an entry reads '...three cast sewn of beans and peas... Forty seven acres... on Hann part of them sewn with Hull beans'. The Hann was that part of Barrow parish that was either pasture or arable depending on local needs, and we see that Laurence was buying in beans from Hull across the Humber – probably to provide the variety and vitality that would come with outside seed. In 1735 there is an entry relating to the corn that was held on the farm. It consisted of 30 loads of wheat in the new lathe (barn) and the 'great roome' (sic) and 35 loads of barley in the outer barn and on the helm (a temporary shelter). A load was a measure of about 30 bushels.

What of the size of the farm and the acreage of crops sown? In 1735-6 he had 53 acres of wheat, 47 acres of beans and peas (often sown as a mixed crop) and 57 acres of barley – a total of 157 acres. By 1740 he had a total of 163 acres under crops in similar proportions. Such acreage made Laurence Wilkin one of the larger farmers in the village.

Some of these crops would be used domestically and others would be saved for seed for the following year, but any surplus was sold and there is evidence of this in the diary. In 1736, 96 quarters of barley were sold for £88 18s 9d (£88 93p) and another ten quarters were sold for £8 15s (£8 75p), giving a price per quarter of around eighteen shillings (90p). Similarly wheat sold for about £1 per quarter. A quarter was a dry measure of eight bushels. These figures are all a little lower than the national average, perhaps indicating that Barrow had enjoyed a better harvest than much of the rest of the country, despite the wet summer of 1736 with its resultant depressed corn prices. The corn was generally sold to local people whose names were all familiar within Barrow, except for some of his wheat which was purchased by Richard Eles[5] (sic) of Hull. It would appear that Laurence Wilkin had a local and regular client base within the village for his cereals.

Using the prices obtained for the crops together with those for wool, we can make an educated guess at the income of the farm for the years 1736 and 1737. In 1736 crops brought in some £141 3s 9d (£141.18p) and wool £10 12s (£10.60p), making a total of £151 15s 9d (£151.78p). In 1737 crops fetched £113 3s 3d (£113.16p) and wool £10 19s (£10.95p), making the yearly total £124 2s 3d (£124.11p). This was on a farm of about 160 acres.

Wages & Personnel
In the eighteenth century, farm workers were broadly divided into two groups. There were the farm servants who were traditionally hired for the year at an agreed wage, with some degree of board and lodging included as part of their payment, and there were those labourers who were hired either on a daily basis or for specific tasks such as harvest and hay mowing. Laurence Wilkin utilised both kinds on his farm. Annual farm servants were traditionally hired at the 'Statas Fairs' which in Lincolnshire were usually held at Martinmas and Mayday, the former coinciding with the slack period after the harvest, and the latter similarly after the lambing season.

Wages, although supposedly laid down by statute, varied considerably across the country according to age, sex and experience of workers, with boys and women usually receiving less than the men did. Wages were agreed at the hiring and paid on a quarterly basis at each of the quarter days. We see from the diary that Laurence Wilkin was providing payment of board and lodge for his living-in servants in the form of raw materials for food and in clothing. There are many entries relating to small sums of money lent to workers throughout the year, and instances of the purchase of gloves, boots, clothing, etc, all of which were carefully added up and deducted from the quarterly wage due, the balance being paid on the quarter day. In 1733 Mary Tomson *(sic)* was paid £2 10s (£2 50p) for her year's work and Esebel *(sic)* Bartel £1 10s (£1 50p), whereas at the other end of the scale, John Bartel received £9 per year as shepherd. John Bartel was the Wilkin's shepherd for several years, receiving between £9 and £10 10s (£10.50p) each year. He was particularly well paid as his position as shepherd was one of great standing. Interestingly in 1741, the year following the disastrous outbreak of sheep rot, John Healey was employed as shepherd at the yearly wage of only £4 10s (£4.50p). Perhaps the rate depended on the number of sheep one looked after. Laurence Wilkin was paying wages that compared quite favourably with those paid in other parts of the country, and with the national average for the period.

Traditionally, a shilling a day was considered the 'going rate' for farm labourers and in 1733 James Melton received £1 16s for six week's work on the harvest. This equates to thirty-six shillings for thirty-six days, if we assume his working week to be one of six days. James Melton was indeed getting a shilling a day.

As well as general work about the farm, specialised work was sometimes necessary and this is illustrated in the entries relating to the blacksmith, Robert Achey. Over several days in May and June 1741, he carried out various tasks on the farm for which he was paid as follows:[6]

May 30	*thone new sho and irons lining*	*1s (5p)*
June 6th	*two remove and two removes*	
	[replacing horse shoes]	*8d (3p)*
June 13th	*2 removes and 2 new shoues*	*8d (3p)*
June 16th	*a dorband and whel barrow bolt mend*	*2d (1p)*
	A half a pund of nales and close gate stapels mend	*8d (3p)*
	A new fork	*1s (5p)*
June 17th	*a share* [plough share] *making and one remove*	*10d (4p)*
June 23rd	*half a pund of nales, 4 wane cloutes*	*1s 4d (7p)*
June 25th	*for one tugteem mending*	*4d (2p)*
June 26th	*for 2 removes and a new sole*	*2d (1p)*
June 28th	*for 2 removes and wane mending*	*4d (2p)*

This work totals up to 7s 2d (36p) out of an agreed quote of £5 for the year's work (1741), but it shows how indispensable the blacksmith was to a working farm.

The farm employed several hands each year and many were used over and over again. Their surnames tell us that the majority of the farm workers were, as one might expect, local people. Out of the thirty names of farmhands in the diary, sixteen were resident in Barrow itself, and of the men, eleven out of twenty were local, and of the women, seven out of ten lived in the village. It would appear that Laurence had a group of regular hands he could call upon each year, plus a selection of people he used only once or twice, whether they were local or otherwise.

Conclusion

It would appear that Laurence Wilkin ran a farm of around 150 to 160 acres in strips scattered throughout the open fields of Barrow in the traditional way, but with at least one enclosed piece of ground out in the East Hann. His farm was mixed, as was the norm at this time, growing wheat and rye, barley and pulses in approximately equal amounts and running a large flock of 200 or more sheep. The whole farming system at this period was communally run, and regulated by the manorial courts in the village according to the laws laid down in the Town Book that had survived from at least the sixteenth century. The farm provided a good living for the Wilkin family, as well as work for between six and seven regular farmhands and numerous day labourers.

The eighteenth century was a period of labour intensive farming using live-in servants and casual labour. The Agricultural Revolution, with its mechanisation and specialisation, was beginning to stir but had yet to reach fruition, and the advent of specialised nitrogen fixing and winter fodder crops was still some way in the future.

The use of three, approximately equal acreages of crops, shows us that Barrow was utilising its four open fields in a three-field system. This would mean three of the fields were under crops and the fourth was laid fallow to recover its fertility, just as one might expect of an integrated open field community, even though, by this period, many similar villages were finding it increasingly difficult to leave a quarter of their land fallow every year.

It was this pressure on land that played some part in the move to enclose such parishes as Barrow-upon-Humber and, indeed, Barrow itself was enclosed between 1797 and 1803. Enclosure destroyed a system that had survived for innumerable generations, giving us the landscape that was all too familiar – until the increasingly mechanised farming practises of the late twentieth century did away with the hedges that the enclosure commissioners had put in place in 1797. Post-enclosure farming did, however, allow for a more individualistic approach to farming and the introduction of newer and more varied crops without the constraints that communal farming imposed.

Notes and References

1 Eagle-eyed readers will notice the variations in the spelling of Wilkin/Wilkyn evident in the article. The very early instances of the surname were spelt with a 'y', gradually changing to the more accepted 'i' version during the eighteenth century. Of course, the spelling was not standardised until the mid-nineteenth century and both versions were equally correct. Some time ago, the author decided to revert to one of the original spellings and had his surnamed changed back to Wilkyn. If nothing else, he says, it will serve to confuse future genealogists.
2 Will of John Wilkyn 1596. *Lincolnshire Archives Office, ref. LCC Wills 1596/66.*
3 *Barrow Town Book*, Lincs. *Lincolnshire Archives Office ref. Barrow Parish 10/1.*
4 Cooke G, *The Complete English Farmer*, London, 1975 p.58.
5 Probably 'Ellis'.
6 Spelling is as found in the diary.

11. THE COASTAL AIRFIELDS OF LINCOLNSHIRE

by Patrick Otter

HIGH ON THE SEA FRONT at Cleethorpes stands a solitary bronze figure of a wartime airman (Figure 1). He is dressed ready for battle, his parachute held casually in his left hand, maps neatly rolled under his arm. His eyes are fixed forever on the distant horizon of the North Sea.

The figure, which stands on High Cliff close to the town's Royal Air Force Association Headquarters, was erected to commemorate over 200 men from the nearby airfield at North Coates who failed to

Figure 1. The lone airman who will forever gaze out to sea from the High Cliff at Cleethorpes. *Author's collection*

Figure 2. All that remained of the First World War Royal Navy Air Station at Killingholme in 1977. This wooden ramp was used for launching seaplanes into the Humber. *Author's collection*

return from operations in the later stages of the war. But for many, the figure has come to commemorate all who lost their lives on operations from the forty-six wartime airfields of Lincolnshire. Not for nothing did Lincolnshire become known as Britain's 'bomber county' half a century ago, and its airfields and squadrons accounted for almost forty per cent of Bomber Command's 55,000 casualties.

Lincolnshire's association with military flying goes back to the wood-and-wire days before the First World War – a conflict that was to see the establishment of numerous airstrips in the coountry, mainly for training purposes. A few of these airstrips were to play a major role in the country's aerial defences as the war went on, including a major seaplane base at North Killingholme on the shores of the Humber. In the latter days of the conflict, this base was used by the Americans who operated both seaplanes (Figure 2) and airships on convoy protection patrols. It was in this same estuary that the first rudimentary trials were carried out, using a converted Humber ferry on what was eventually to become a major weapon of war – the aircraft carrier.

The Armistice in 1918 brought a rapid run-down in military aviation activity in Lincolnshire, and it was not until the mid-1930s, when it was evident that a freshly bellicose Germany posed a new threat to European peace, that the country once again began to see an airfield expansion. As a coastal county, it was evident that Lincolnshire would be in the front line of any new war. Airfields were planned with that in mind.

The great Airfield Expansion Scheme, put in train around 1935, included the redevelopment of existing airfields and the building of a string of new ones. Most were situated on the higher grounds of the Wolds or along the Lincolnshire Cliff, but one, Manby near Louth, was on the flat coastal plain, and a second on the site of the old landing strip at North Coates abutted the dunes bordering the North Sea.

These airfields (the others included Waddington, Scampton, Hemswell, Binbrook, Coningsby, Digby, Kirton Lindsey and Swinderby) were all big, brick-built places, providing spacious hangarage and comfortable living quarters for those who were to serve there.

Opened between 1936 and 1941, these major airfields were merely the forerunners of the huge wartime building programme put into operation in the late summer of 1940. This led to a building programme the like of which Lincolnshire had never seen before, or has ever seen since. Airfields, most of them designed for heavy bomber operations, sprang up everywhere from the Fens to the Wolds, from the coastal marshes to the Trent. They were, in comparison to their pre-war cousins, rough and ready affairs: corrugated iron hangars and Nissen huts, prefabricated buildings and concrete runways, and hardstanding for bombers. The pace of construction matched the urgency of the times: RAF Ludford Magna, 400 feet up on the Wolds, took a little over ninety days to build compared with the two years or more spent on the careful construction of Manby. Little wonder that few traces of Ludford remain, while Manby continues to be a landmark on the Lincolnshire Marsh.

The coastal strip bordering the lower reaches of the Humber and Gibraltar Point, where the North Sea gives way to the Wash, was not ideal airfield-building country but the Air Ministry surveyors, in their wisdom, identified a number of sites. New airfields were built at Goxhill, North Killingholme (just inland from the old seaplane station), Waltham and Strubby. Other sites, too, were redeveloped. Donna Nook became the most coastal of all landing strips when it was used as a satellite for the Coastal Command airfield at North Coates; Sutton Bridge, which bordered the Wash in the extreme south of the county, was a major training airfield for fighter pilots; Wainfleet, Holbeach and Theddlethorpe all became vitally important ranges for Bomber Command. There were, of course, many other airfields just inland: Elsham Wolds, Kirmington, Binbrook, Kelstern, Spilsby and the rest, but here we will confine ourselves to those on, or very near, the Lincolnshire coast.

This coastline was to play an ever-increasingly important part in the lives of the young aircrews from all parts of the world who were to serve in the county between 1939 and 1945. The Mablethorpe area was one of the primary assembly points for the great bomber streams of 1943 and onwards. Hundreds upon hundreds of Lancasters from Lincolnshire, and Halifaxes from Yorkshire, would rise in a mighty spiral before heading out over the North Sea. Lincolnshire's coastline was also a hugely welcome sight for many as they nursed battered bombers back from the night skies of Germany; for thousands more, it was to be their very last sight of the free world.

A prime Luftwaffe target

The most northerly of all Lincolnshire's airfields was at **Goxhill**, less than a mile from the broad expanse of the upper Humber estuary. During the First World War, the Royal Flying Corps used a couple of fields near the village as a landing ground and, doubtless, this is what drew Air Ministry surveyors to the site early in 1940. They identified land to the east of the village as suitable for one of the string of new bomber airfields planned for Lincolnshire and construction work began early in 1941. By that time, however, fate had overtaken the role Goxill was to play in the war.

Goxhill lies less than four miles, as the crow flies, from Hull – a city that had become a prime target for the Luftwaffe during 1941. Its docks were of major importance to the British war effort and its location, at the head of a wide and easily-distinguishable estuary, ensured it received frequent and heavy raids and, among counter measures taken to protect the city, was the siting of barrage balloons attached to lighters moored in the Humber. These were intended to deter the low level attacks often favoured by the Germans, but they also had the effect of ending any prospect of Goxhill being used by RAF bombers.

By this time, work at Goxhill was nearing completion and the airfield had already been allocated to Bomber Command's No. 1 Group. The only use that could be found for the airfield was as a base for one of its target towing flights. Instead of the anticipated squadron of Wellington bombers, Goxhill found itself host to half a dozen drogue-towing Lysanders.

However, during the spring of 1942, the airfield was visited by an advance party from the American 8th Air Force, due to move to England that summer. Apart from the operational airfields allocated in East Anglia, the 8th was looking for somewhere to fine-hone the training of its fighter pilots in European conditions. Goxhill fitted the bill almost exactly.

Within a matter of weeks, this airfield became the first in Britain to be handed over to the Americans, in a ceremony attended by Air Marshal Sir Charles Portal and General Dwight D Eisenhower. Days later, a special train arrived at the local station carrying hundreds of young Americans to staff the new airfield. Their arrival sparked a new flurry of activity as facilities at Goxhill, deemed to be perfectly adequate for the Royal Air Force, were immediately upgraded for the newcomers, unused as they were to the rigours of life on a wartime British airfield.

The first US aircraft to arrive were P38 Lightnings of the 71st Fighter Squadron, flying to Britain via Nova Scotia, Greenland and Iceland. They were destined for service in North Africa but spent time at Goxhill getting used to European conditions. Few of the initial batch of pilots were to survive their first experience of action against the Me109s in North Africa, but the Americans that followed proved to be quick learners.

Over the next two years, hundreds of 8th Air Force fighter pilots were to pass through Goxhill's tough training regime, at first flying P38s, P39 Airacobras and ex-RAF Spitfires, then later P47

Figure 3. Over here! Young Americans at Goxhill in front of a P51 Mustang, 1944. *Author's collection*

Thunderbolts and the superb P51 Mustangs (Figure 3). From Goxhill (known universally to the Americans who served there as Goathill), they mainly flew training sorties, although the station records show that aircraft from Goxhill occasionally joined RAF patrols along the North Sea coast. A total of twenty-three pilots were killed in training accidents at Goxhill, accidents that accounted for some fifty-three aircraft.

The pilots' stay at Goxhill may have been brief, but the large American staff at the airfield certainly left its mark on the local community – several local girls became GI brides, while in nearby Grimsby, a drapery store was converted into an American Red Cross club for the use of the Goxhill airmen and the American soldiers who spent some time at Immingham.

The Americans moved out early in 1945 and Goxhill was handed back to the RAF. It was then used mainly for storage purposes before it finally closed. The airfield largely escaped the ravages of post-war redevelopment and much of what was built almost sixty years ago can still be seen, making Goxhill one of the best preserved of all Lincolnshire's wartime airfields.

A few miles south lies what remains of RAF **North Killingholme**, now an industrial estate servicing the nearby port of Immingham, but once, briefly, it was the home of 550 Squadron and its Lancaster bombers. The airfield lies so close to the Humber that, when 550 Squadron first arrived on a very wet morning on 3 January 1944, its aircraft crews could be forgiven for thinking the airfield was actually in the river. Huge pools of water stood between the newly laid runways and the muddy islands housing hastily built accommodation and technical sites.

North Killingholme was a perfect example of a hurriedly constructed wartime airfield: cold, uncomfortable, shoddy – but supremely efficient. It was to be the home of that single Lancaster squadron, 550, which flew operationally from there until the war in Europe ended. It may have been a brief tenure, but it was also a dramatic one. The squadron took part in 192 raids (Figure 4), mounted 3,582 sorties, and lost just fifty-nine aircraft – one of the lowest loss rates in Bomber Command. During that time, 550 squadron regularly figures at, or near, the top of the bombing 'charts', establishing an all-time record by dropping 1,534 tons of bombs in March 1945.

There was also the distinction of being credited with the opening assault on the Normandy beaches on 6 June 1944. One of 550's Lancasters, LL811 J-Jig, known as *Bad Penny II* to its crew, dropped

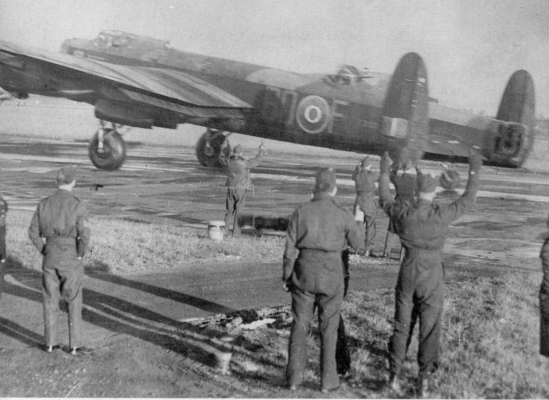

Figure 4. Come back safely! Lancaster F-Freddie is waved away by her ground crew as she prepares to take off for a daylight raid from North Killingholme in 1944. *Author's collection*

the first bombs to herald the opening of the invasion. Its crew members later received a collective *Croix de Guerre* from the French government to mark their achievement; the illuminated plaque also presented to them now hangs in the local church.

This squadron's secret of success was its leadership and the quality of its men. There was a fierce *esprit de corps*, even though it was among the last to be formed in Bomber Command. That spirit is still alive today, for each year 550's dwindling band of veterans still gather for their annual reunion at St Denys' Church which, although in the neighbouring parish of East Halton, actually overlooks the old airfield. This reunion custom is carried out at many of the county's airfields, and an honoured guest to them all (weather and other commitments permitting) is the RAF's last flying Lancaster, PA474 – the *City of Lincoln*. Every year, it makes several low-level passes over a reunion airfield or roadside memorial before dipping its wings as a salute to the men and their families watching through tear-misted eyes from below.

The squadron that served so faithfully at North Killingholme was formed in the late autumn of 1943, at another Bomber Command Airfield close to Lincolnshire's coast – **Waltham**, situated just south of Grimsby. Waltham was the home of 100 Squadron and in December 1943, its C Flight was detached to form the nucleus of 550, taking with it its aircrew, ground crew and Lancasters.

Waltham's official name was RAF Grimsby, but it was known universally by the name of the village it adjoined. The airfield site, lying between Waltham itself and the neighbouring village of Holton-le-Clay, had been used for private flying since the early 1930s, first as the home of the Lincolnshire Flying Club and then, later, as Grimsby's municipal airport.

The site was a natural acquisition for the Air Ministry in May 1940. Work began almost immediately on the construction of a bomber airfield, complete with hardened runways that were pressed into use, almost as soon as the concrete had dried, by nearby RAF Binbrook. The latter had been completed in the spring that same year as one of the Expansion Scheme airfields, without the benefit of hardened runways so, when its resident squadrons exchanged their light Fairey Battles for much heavier Wellingtons during the winter of 1940, they had been restricted to flying operationally only when the ground was hard enough to take the weight of their bomb-laden aircraft.

Waltham was designated as a satellite of Binbrook and one of its two Wellington squadrons, 142, began operating from there as soon as the runways were usable. In November 1941, when the airfield formally opened, 142 officially moved in, flying from there for the next year before moving to North Africa. It was replaced almost immediately by 100 Squadron that had just returned to England after flying torpedo bombers in the Far East. The squadron re-formed on Lancasters at Waltham and flew its first operation a few weeks later, dropping mines off the French coast.

100 Squadron was to remain at Waltham for the rest of the war, flying more than 4,000 sorties and losing 113 Lancasters, 92 of them on operations. Waltham's worst night of the war came in December 1943, when its bombers returned from a heavy attack on Berlin, only to find their airfield (along with others in Lincolnshire) shrouded in fog. As they tried to land, two of the aircraft collided in mid-air over the airfield, a third crashed nearby, and a fourth flew into the Lincolnshire Wolds while trying to land at Kelstern. Just five of the twenty-eight men on board these aircraft survived. The dead included 100 Squadron's young Commanding Officer, Wing Commander David Holford.

Figure 5. Lancaster J-Jug of 100 Squadron at Waltham in 1944. The aircraft carried the name *Jug and Bottle* on its nose and is now commemorated in a public house built approximately on this spot. *Author's collection*

But 100 squadron had its good times, too – particularly during the autumn of 1944 when it lost just one aircraft in a four-month period. Four of the squadron's Lancasters also achieved the distinction of recording over 100 operations. 100 Squadron moved out of Waltham in April 1945, and the airfield closed.

Post-war attempts to revive civilian flying came to nothing; now only scattered parts of the airfield remain. A memorial to those who served there stands alongside the A16 close to the airfield boundary, while in Holton-le-Clay, a pub, built on the site of one of the old dispersal pans has been named after a Lancaster that had once stood there – *Jug and Bottle* (Figure 5).

Allocated to Coastal Command

Of all the wartime coastal airfields in Lincolnshire, none was closer to the sea than RAF **North Coates** (Figure 6). It was also one of the most significant, serving a crucial role in Coastal Command's operations against German shipping in the North Sea.

The site, originally known as North Coast Fitties, had been in use

Figure 6. British and German war graves in the churchyard at North Coates. *Author's collection*

during the First World War, then later as an armaments practice camp by the RAF. Extensively redeveloped in the late 1930s, it was still used as a training establishment until February 1940, when it was allocated to Coastal Command. Further extension work was carried out, including the laying of a single 1,400 feet concrete runway. Work was still going on when the first flying units moved in, three squadrons of Blenheims that provided long-distance patrols over the North Sea. These were quickly replaced by Beaufort torpedo bombers of 22 Squadron and Fleet Air Arm Swordfishes of 812, the only biplanes to see operational service in Lincolnshire during the war. Both units were at North Coates that summer when the airfield was visited by Winston Churchill as part of his inspection of the county's anti-invasion defences.

By that autumn, the Beauforts of 22 Squadron were in action, sinking their first German shipping off the Frisian Islands. Pilots included Flying Officer Kenneth Campbell, who was to win a posthumous Victoria Cross for his part in an attack on the battlecruiser *Gneisenau* in the Port of Brest, in April 1941. His torpedo crippled the warship before his aircraft was shot down. Campbell's aircraft had been one of nine detached from North Coates to St Eval in Cornwall specifically for this operation.

Eventually, the Beauforts of 22 Squadron were replaced at North Coates by the Hudsons of 86 and 407 (RCAF) Squadrons. They conducted anti-shipping patrols over the North Sea, attacking mainly German coastal convoys. New tactics introduced into Coastal Command operations saw the formation of the powerful North Coates Wing: three squadrons of Beaufighters, two equipped with cannon-firing aircraft and the third with torpedoes. The idea was that the first two would be used to suppress German flak ships before the third went in to launch torpedo attacks. After an uncertain beginning, the North Coates Wing (which later included rocket-firing Beaufighters) dominated much of the North Sea, virtually closing it off to German shipping (Figure 7).

The final operation of the war, in April 1945, saw aircraft from

Figure 7. Beaufighters of the North Coates Strike Wing attack a German convoy off the Frisian Islands, 1944. *Peter Green collection*

North Coates sink six U-boats and five merchant ships, with damage to a further two. It was, indeed, a dramatic finale.

After the war, North Coates was used, like many other Lincolnshire airfields, to store some of the thousands of tons of surplus RAF equipment. Later, it was used as the base for the first helicopter air-sea rescue unit on the east coast, and then for housing ground-to-air Bloodhound missiles – before finally closing. Much of the airfield remains today, and it is still used by a very active flying club.

A few miles down the coast, RAF **Donna Nook** had for some years been used as a relief landing ground. Although it had few facilities, its grass runways were pressed into use by North Coates to help ease its own overcrowding. At times, Donna Nook, was used operationally, with aircraft being prepared for raids at North Coates. They were then flown to Donna Nook, as part of their air-testing, before being flown operationally. This enabled the North Coates squadrons to launch and recover all its aircraft quickly – an important element in mounting operations over the North Sea.

Tragically, Donna Nook was to witness one of the worst accidents on a wartime airfield in Lincolnshire on the night of 22 January 1942. Several Hudsons had left the airstrip for a raid on shipping off Borkum, but the attack was cancelled. As they returned, one aircraft crash-landed, bursting into flames. Rescuers were trying to reach the five men trapped inside when the aircraft's bombs exploded, killing them, along with another eleven RAF personnel and two soldiers from the airfield defence force. Another sixteen men were seriously injured.

Apart from its landing strip, Donna Nook was also the control centre for one of the four major wartime bombing ranges on the Lincolnshire coast. It was centred on Somercotes Haven, which had been used as a gunnery and bombing range by aircraft using the armament camps at North Coates since the 1920s. In 1940, the range passed to the control of Bomber Command's No 1 Group, based in North Lincolnshire. It was used by their Lancasters and Wellingtons for the remainder of the war.

The RAF maintained a post-war presence at Donna Nook and its bombing range was reopened in the early 1970s for NATO aircraft. It quickly became so heavily used that it developed into a popular tourist attraction, complete with its own car park, viewing area and resident ice-cream seller!

A second range, a few miles further south at **Theddlethorpe**, was opened primarily to serve the wartime Air Armament School established at nearby RAF Manby. This range remained open after the war, finally closing with the construction of the nearby North Sea gas terminal.

Manby, itself, was the wartime academy of armament training within the Royal Air Force. It was at this large pre-war station, a few miles inland from Mablethorpe, that gunners, bomb aimers and armament officers learned the skills that were to serve them so well in the bomber campaign.

Work on the airfield began as part of the Expansion Scheme in 1936 and the station opened some two years later as the RAF's No 1 Air Armament school (Figure 8). This school brought with it a whole host of aircraft, most of them long-obsolete biplanes. The early war years also saw the formation of the No 1 Ground Armament School at Manby and this, in turn, led to further expansion of its facilities.

Manby was the first airfield in Lincolnshire to be built with a concrete runway but, by 1943, it had become so busy that two more runways were laid. Around this time, the Air Armament School was expanded to become the Empire Central Armament School, a unit given the task of further developing the gunnery and bomb-aiming skills of Bomber Command. Later in the war this unit, which was of sufficient importance to be led by an air commodore, became the Empire Air Armament School. Its biplanes had long since given way to Blenheims, Hudsons, Wellingtons and, eventually, Lancasters and

Figure 8. Hangars under construction at Manby in the winter of 1936. *Author's collection*

a single Mosquito.

Manby retained its value to the Royal Air Force long after the war. In 1949, the RAF Flying College was formed there while, in 1951, it became the headquarters of 25 Group, whose role was to oversee the training of crews for the jet age. The Flying College became the College of Air Warfare in 1962 and remained at Manby until the airfield closed in 1974.

Shortly afterwards, parts of the airfield were acquired as the headquarters of the then new East Lindsey District Council. Still at this site, the Council is housed in the appropriately named Tedder Hall.

The final airfield on our coastal journey is to be found near the small village of **Strubby**, some four miles from the sea south-west of Mablethorpe. It was very much the bomber airfield that nearly never was.

This site, which lay between Strubby and its neighbouring parish of Woodthorpe, was one of those identified by the Air Ministry in 1940 as suitable for airfield construction, but it was some three years later before the builders finally got round to it. Intended as yet another airfield for Bomber Command's 5 Group, by the time it was ready for occupation in April 1944, it had no use for Strubby. However, plans were afoot for the reorganisation of airfields in Lincolnshire later in the year and so, in the meantime, Strubby was loaned to Coastal Command.

For a few brief weeks, the airfield boasted its own Beaufighter Strike Wing that operated in conjunction with the North Coates Wing (Figure 9), and proved devastatingly effective in preventing any wide scale use by the Germans of the North Sea during those crucial weeks following the Normandy Landings.

Briefly, the Beaufighter squadrons, 144 and 404 (RCAF), shared Strubby with a third coastal squadron, 280, which flew Warwicks in an air-sea rescue role. These aircraft, a variant of the Wellington that carried 'Lindholme' lifeboats in their converted bomb bays, saved the lives of many young airmen.

The Coastal Command squadrons moved out in September 1944 to make way for the Lancasters of 619 Squadron. There were so many airfields around Lincoln that their previous home, Dunholme Lodge, had been closed to flying and the squadron moved to Strubby, its final wartime home. Its Lancasters operated from the new airfield for the first time on 4 October when five aircraft sowed mines close to a U-boat base in Oslo fjord. Ironically, 619's last wartime operation was to drop mines in exactly the same area.

A second Lancaster squadron, 227, was formed at Strubby that

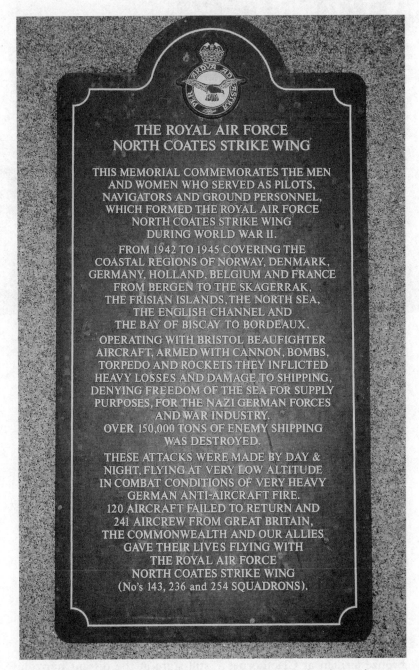

Figure 9. The plaque on the statue plinth commemorating those who were lost flying with the North Coates Strike Wing from 1942 until 1945. *Author's collection*

Figure 10. The watchtower at RAF Strubby pictured soon after the airfield closed. The 'greenhouse' on the top was a post-war addition. *Author's collection*

autumn before moving to Balderton, near Newark. It was to return to share Strubby with 619 for the final few weeks of the war.

Losses from Strubby were low, but 619 had the misfortune to lose one of the last Lancasters shot down in the war as well as having the last Group 5 casualty. The aircraft, D-Dumbo, was brought down by anti-aircraft fire in an attack on Bertchesgarden on 25 April 1945. Only three of its crew survived. It was the 3,358th Lancaster lost on operations by Bomber Command.

Strubby remained in use as a satellite of RAF Manby until 1974 when it closed. Just a handful of buildings and a few strips of runway survive as a reminder of RAF Strubby's brief role in Lincolnshire's air war (Figure 10).

They will always remember

Today, the Lincolnshire coastline still reverberates to the sound of military aviation, although now only a handful of its airfields are still active. The region is still visited by the veterans of 1939-45, who make their annual pilgrimage to places such as Wickenby, Skellingthorpe, Metheringham and Ludford Magna. When they arrive, they – like the bronze airman at Cleethorpes – still stare at the distant horizon and think of times past and the men who never made it back.

12. A Brief Look at Grimsby's Fishing Heritage

by Jenny Walton

JUSTLY PROUD OF ITS REPUTATION as Europe's Food Town, Great Grimsby actually has a long heritage of food association, going back to those early days when the first people who settled in the area farmed the nearby Humber and North Sea, both for their own sustenance and for trading. However, the actual fishing industry that was to make Grimsby an international name remained comparatively small for generations, whilst commercial enterprise from its port steadily strengthened.

Although the town may never have existed without its water-borne trade, it may also be true that: 'If it weren't for Grimsby, we might never have seen the white beard of Captain Birdseye' and that it was this selfsame Captain '…(or someone close to him) who invented the fish finger, and it was Grimsby which produced the first frozen pea'.[1] Grimsby originally depended upon a harbour that could be accessed by Scandinavian longships; it was not possible to accommodate any larger type of vessel at that time. Its haven, whose course ran roughly north to south (Figure 1), was fed by springs rising near the Humber Estuary. In the early Middle Ages, the haven was tidal to points now more than a mile from high-water mark, its navigable part ending where today's Victoria Street Riverhead is situated (although it once flowed a short distance further south along the eastern boundary of the town). The River Freshney, which joined the Humber without entering the town itself, also had a haven just a short distance beyond the town boundary.

By the end of the Middle Ages, the town was sited on a flat, low-lying peninsula extending northwards to the tidal waters of the haven, hemmed in by salt marshes as far south as Salt Ings to the west, and eastwards to an area between the abbey and Weelsby, of which the People's Park now forms part. Grimsby was connected to the rest of Lincolnshire by the turnpike, a single-track road running north and south (now known as Bargate).

Documentation[2] shows a number of references to the local fishing industry and related problems that have arisen over the years; the infamous Cod Wars were far from the first disputes to affect the area.

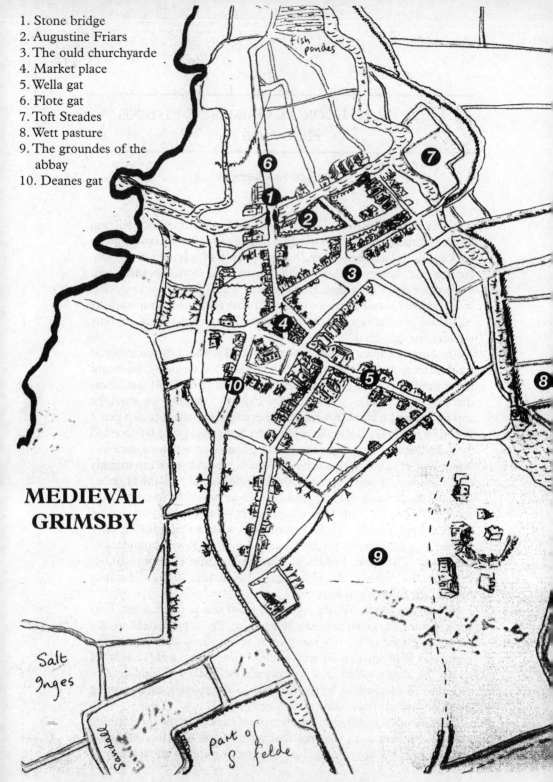

1. Stone bridge
2. Augustine Friars
3. The ould churchyarde
4. Market place
5. Wella gat
6. Flote gat
7. Toft Steades
8. Wett pasture
9. The groundes of the abbay
10. Deanes gat

MEDIEVAL GRIMSBY

Salt gnges

part of S felde

Figure 1. The haven waterway, which can be seen running from the top middle of the map, past 'fish pondes', to just below half way down the right-hand side of the map, is where the modern-day Alexandra Dock is situated. Where it forks to the left, it can be seen running underneath an iron bridge on 'Flote gat', now Alexandra Road. This fork is now known as the West Haven, which lies alongside Frederick Ward Way. *From an original map of Grimsby, courtesy of North East Lincolnshire Council, Grimsby Reference Library.*

As far back as 1201 there was an argument – between the Abbot of Wellow (the local man), who claimed to hold the tithes on fish landed on this part of the coast, and the Prior of Bridlington (in Yorkshire), concerning fishermen of Filey landing their catches at Grimsby. There was also a fourteenth century feud between Grimsby and the neighbouring thorpes of Clee, Oole and Itterby. As fishermen did not have to pay tolls for anchorage and quayage at Grimsby, as decreed in a charter granted by Edward I (1272-1307), it was a preferred landing place for catches. A subsequent trial in Westminster Court in 1326 resulted in the verdict being given in favour of Grimsby, to the disgust of the residents of the contesting thorpes who claimed the fishing rights from time immemorial.

Another medieval dispute concerned Grimsby merchants. They strongly objected to the wiles of Ravenserod people whose port was sited at the mouth of the Humber, near Spurn Point and who encouraged trade away from Grimsby, by inducing fishing vessels to land at their quay, and then detaining them for so long that the catch would have turned rotten before they could have reached Grimsby; a crafty way of ensuring the catch would have to stay at Ravenserod. They would also offer double the prices that Grimsby could, thus affecting Grimsby's markets. It was said that Divine Right stepped in, however, when, in 1341, Ravenserod was washed away by the sea.

A tithing arrangement was made in 1305 by the Abbot of Wellow with Walter Bell, and Walter, son of Richard Storme of Itterby in the parish of St Savior of Clee, whereby the two Walters undertook to mark every fifteenth fish they caught at sea or in the Humber with cords, lines or nets. If they sold the catch in some other port, the Abbot was to have a fifteenth of the value of the whole catch – including conger eels, salmon, porpoises and turtles.

The town's first dock

Henry III's grants of tolls to Grimsby in 1255 and 1261 had included repairs for the port. In 1280, when quayage was granted for three years, there were complaints that the haven was so badly silted with mud and sand that vessels experienced extreme difficulty navigating its course; yet it took more than sixty years before anything radical was done to overcome the problem. It had been acknowledged that, in order to keep the haven free of silt, the Freshney would have to be diverted. This proposal had been rejected following concerns regarding potential flooding, received from landowners in Little Coates and Great Coates. However, by 1335, the situation had deteriorated to the extent that the Borough burgesses petitioned the Crown for financial aid to appropriate the King's waste places in the town. By the time the grant was received, in April 1341, an extension to the existing harbour had been created along the town's northern boundary – later to become known as the West Haven.

The Port's proximity to the North Sea and local salt workings made it a popular landing place for visiting fishing boats. There is also evidence of shipbuilding at the Port during the fourteenth century. Hazardous fishing expeditions from Grimsby to Iceland were being made by the fifteenth century. Scottish salmon was landed here, and smokehouses were in existence.

During the sixteenth century, the state of the haven continued to steadily worsen, especially from amassing silt – much of which was attributed to the water mills. Thirty-eight men promised donations up to £12 2s. 4d (£12.11½p) for a pair of cloughs[3] to modify the haven in 1519. A man was paid four shillings (20p) per annum to look after them. However, each year saw a continuing decline in water-borne trade, and, by the financial year 1571-72, the only vessels using the haven were a couple of keels (one transporting turf, the other lime), a crayer with salt, four hoys carrying coal, a Scottish ship with fish, and three other ships. One hundred years later, the waterway was just about still in use, although ships could not travel very far up its creek-like course.

It is known that, during the seventeenth century, fishermen from the nearby Yorkshire ports landed their catches at Grimsby; salmon, too, was still being landed here, as were lobsters from Denmark. As busy as it was, the Port remained of comparatively little importance until 1796, when the Grimsby Haven Company was formed. This Company had been granted powers under the *Grimsby Haven Act* of the same year to 'widen, enlarge, alter and improve the existing haven', thus creating the first enclosed dock – the Old Dock, a water area of approximately fifteen acres.[4] Together with the provision of a lock pit, this was undoubtedly the start of Grimsby's use as a port of some worth to both fishing vessels and commercial shipping.

By the 1840s, the Grimsby Haven Company was experiencing financial difficulties as a result of the lack of transport links outside the immediate hinterland. Fortunately, the Sheffield, Ashton-under-Lyne & Manchester Railway Company was also seeking to establish a terminus on the East Coast so, during September 1844, a meeting was arranged between senior representatives of these companies with a view to take over operation of the Port. Meanwhile, a group of local landowners had decided to build their own railway and form the Great Grimsby and Sheffield Junction (GG&SJ) Company. By the end of 1844, they had come to an agreement with the Haven Company to create the Grimsby Dock Company.

In 1845, the *Dock Act* was passed, thereby allowing the Grimsby Dock Company to acquire the assets of the Haven Company and, in the following year, the *Amalgamation Act* received Royal Assent to bring together the Grimsby Dock Company and the GG&SJ under the Manchester, Sheffield and Lincolnshire Railway (MS & LR) Company.

This new Company embarked upon the building of a new dock at a cost of approximately £1 million, on reclaimed land out in the Humber. Albert, Prince Consort, laid the foundation stone on 18 April 1849, and after a further three years construction work, it opened for business on 27 May 1852. Following a visit from Queen Victoria and Prince Albert on their Royal Yacht, *The Fairy*, in October 1854, the New Dock was renamed the Royal Dock (Figure 2).

Grimsby town's famous landmark, the 309 feet tall Dock Tower was completed in March 1852. Originally designed to provide hydraulic pressure for the operation of the fifteen quayside cranes, six pairs of lock gates and the associated sluices, it now forms a prominent reminder of local Victorian engineering. By

Figure 2. The Royal Dock under construction, from a painting by J W Carmichael. *Courtesy of ABP, Grimsby and Immingham.*

accommodating 30,000 gallons of water in a tank located in the lower of the two balconies, a pressure equal to 100lb per square inch could be achieved. However, in 1892, a small accumulator tower was built on the opposite side of the seventy-foot lock which was able to provide the same result without the height. The introduction of further accumulator towers around the dock, together with the later use of electric or electro-hydraulic energy, has completely ended the employment of the Dock Tower for which it was originally designed. Commercial traffic passing through the Port continued to increase over the succeeding years, resulting in a need for provision of extra berthing space. This was assisted in 1872 when work commenced on the construction of a cutting to connect the Old Dock with the Royal Dock. Officially opened on 22 July 1879 by the Prince and Princess of Wales during their visit to the town, it created a direct link between the two commercial docks, without having to pass through the two main entrance locks from one dock to the other. To mark the occasion, the Old Dock – which was also being extended by another twenty-six acres – was then renamed Alexandra Dock.

Increasing importance of Grimsby Port

The construction of the Great Northern Line to London in the mid-nineteenth century had the greatest influence in turning Grimsby into a major fishing port. This coincided with a time when diminishing yields of fish from traditional grounds led to fishing taking place further north, and Grimsby became the favourite port from which to send the catch, by rail, to London. It was particularly favoured because smacks using the Port of Hull had to be towed to sea if the wind was unfavourable, whereas Grimsby Port was actually on the coast. Additionally, the turn-round time for landing a catch and returning to the fishing grounds was much quicker via Grimsby. Although Grimsby was the site of prolific smack building, between 1853 and 1854 the Railway Company built two steam-line fishing vessels and seven of the first sailing trawlers to operate from its waters. In the following year, John Howard of Manningtree, Essex, was persuaded by the Railway Company to transfer his eight sailing ships to Grimsby, thus giving a tremendous boost to the size and importance of the local trawling fleet.

At first, smacks used both the town's docks, but the construction of a special Fish Dock by the MS & L R, sited east of the Royal Dock, was started in the summer of 1855 and was ready for use by 1856. The six-acre area included a lock-pit, an entrance pier and a thatched ice-house, sited nearby, to which local carters and bargemen were encouraged to collect and deliver ice. During the first year, the tonnage of fish dispatched by rail from Grimsby had doubled to 3,400 tons. As time went by, an increasing proportion of the fish landed here was salted, smoked or consumed locally.

With the introduction of ice, salt, which had been used as a preservative of fish from the very early days, was no longer the main option. It is of interest to note that some early smacks actually kept their catch alive by putting it in wells with holes drilled in the sides through which fresh, salt sea water flowed. Once landed, the fish were then kept alive in floating wooden chests for as long as necessary – until sold or auctioned.

By 1859, the dock had become too small to accommodate the increasing number of fishing vessels visiting the Port. As a result of smack owners petitioning the Railway Company, by the following year the dock had been enlarged by about another six acres, its existing pontoon demolished and a new 200 feet long platform constructed, thereby doubling its size. From the seventeen vessels using Grimsby's fish-landing facilities in 1857, the figure grew to 112 by 1863.

As trade continued to rise, the demand for additional facilities increased. In 1870, the Railway Company had constructed No 2 Fish Dock, thereby creating a further eight acres of water area. By 1900, this had been extended to sixteen acres, thereby providing a total of twenty-nine acres of enclosed water space within the Number 1 and Number 2 Fish Docks.

Importing ice from Norway

The first two cargoes of ice from Norway arrived in the Port in March 1857, enabling many fishing vessels to make trips loaded with lump ice in order to keep the catch fresh. By 1876, Grimsby was handling about 50,000 tons of ice from Norway each year.

As the importation of Norwegian block ice developed, a group of Grimsby owners formed the Grimsby Ice Company in order to produce ice on the Dock Estate. A successful venture, the demand was so heavy that, by the turn of the nineteenth century, it was described as the largest ice producing factory in the world. Messrs. Hagerup and Doughty followed with an ice-making factory in Robinson Street (later used for cold storage purposes, and demolished in 1991). A third factory was built in Victor Street for the Standard Steam Fishing and Ice Company. This also was used for cold storage, until closed down and re-opened for religious, entertainment and retail purposes.

Grimsby's dependence on the fishing industry

As the nineteenth century moved into its second half, the growth of Grimsby's fishing industry accelerated, and people started arriving from all over the country to take advantage of a lucrative employment, within, or related to the industry. Fish merchants were making fortunes and began taking part in local government – the first was elected in 1853 and, within twenty years, four of the sixteen councillors were smack owners.

By 1869, the economy of the town was almost completely dependent on the fishing industry, with 3,400 men and boys going to sea in smacks, and another 100 sailing in steam carriers and ice-barques. Vessel maintenance and construction employed another 564; there were 400 men and women working in 41 smokehouses, 400 labourers on the pontoon where the fish was landed and sold, and another 161 employed by ancillary companies.

Apprentices were in great demand, too, as the industry throve. Although local boys were used, most came from such public bodies as orphanages, industrial schools, prisoners' aid societies, children's homes, foundling hospitals and reformatories. Apprenticeship lasted for between five and six years, with lads starting as young as twelve years of age and earning around ten to fourteen shillings (50p-70p) a week. It was a hard life for the youngsters, and not all of them saw their apprenticeship as a career opportunity. Many ran away, but, when caught, were usually sent to prison in chains for anywhere between ten days and six weeks. Many preferred the risk of imprisonment, however, than dicing with death whilst at sea where, ignorance and, very often, lack of supervision, led to great loss of life. Swabbing the decks was particularly hazardous, as a sudden swell of the sea could wash a boy over the side of the two-foot high bulwarks, or they could fall from the rigging whilst putting up or taking down the sidelights.

By 1877, trawlers and others using Grimsby Port were employing around 1,680 fishermen and 1,790 apprentice boys[5] – but the number of the latter was now decreasing in availability. Consequently, weekly hands were employed, a type of labour considered inferior to the apprentices. Another 5,099 people were employed in associated work on the docks.

The following year, the Fisheries Institute was built in Orwell Street to provide technical education for all fishermen, as well as hot baths, swimming baths, and some social facilities. Tuition on nautical subjects was also available there, so that those with little education could become more proficient fishermen.

Many skippers were illiterate, too, and unable to keep a log, nor did they have much understanding of the principals of navigation; they plotted a course round the fishing grounds by depth-sounding with a lead weight. This lack of seafaring knowledge became more of a problem when vessels began sailing further north in order to find sufficient fish – longer trips into somewhat unknown territory were dangerous and needed skippers of greater ability. So, the *Board of Trade Order* of 1880 stated that although serving skippers or mates would be given certificates of servitude, further applicants would be expected to undergo an oral examination. To meet these new conditions, courses were offered at the Fisher Lads' Institute. Another change in the old, accepted ways came about with the *Merchant Shipping Act* of 1880, where a ruling decreed that men or boys should not be imprisoned for desertion.

The following year, the Great Grimsby Trawling Company was formed.

The 1893-1899 Cod War

The introduction of steam trawlers and their ability to travel further afield, gave all ship owners confidence to send their vessels as far afield as Iceland. But, as catches from Icelandic grounds grew in size and number, the Danish Government controlling the island claimed a fishing limit of thirteen miles. British trawlers ignored this limit and continued to fish there leading to patrolling Danish gunboats escorting a number of the 'law-breaking' vessels to port where fines were imposed and part or all of both catch and gear was confiscated. Bitterness on both sides lasted until 1896, when Great Britain made an agreement with Iceland that:

> *...allowed for British vessels to shelter and use any Icelandic port provided their gear and trawls were stowed. In return British vessels were not to fish east of a line from Illunypa to Thornodesker Islet.*[6]

Trawlers built during the late nineteenth and early twentieth centuries were quite different from their modern counterparts.

> *The bridge was aft of the funnel, which did not help navigation. On the other hand the position was useful for watching the warps when fishing, and to be able to gauge the depth. The early trawlers had none of the equipment available today which helps the skipper considerably towards a successful fishing trip; no wireless, radar, gyro, electricity. It was hand steering; a magnetic compass; paraffin lamps; candles for the fish room; cork-blocks fitted together for life jackets; no derricks; gear all handled by the crew.*[7]

Fishermen on strike

Between 1885 and 1889, 367 men and boys from Grimsby lost their lives whilst at sea – typical of the high loss of life in the industry. In 1885, fishermen in smacks decided to do something about obtaining better all-round conditions, including being compensated for the long periods they were away from home – often up to six weeks at a time. This was because smacks were being sent out to work as a fleet and carrier ships brought fresh provisions for the seamen, collected the catch and delivered it back to the port. This was a state of affairs that was especially unpleasant during the winter months when the men's only means of warmth came from a small, smoky galley stove, besides being highly dangerous during the transfer of boxes of fish from the numerous smaller vessels having to crowd around the carrier ship.

Inevitably, there was a rebellion. The men refused to go to sea until conditions were improved and trip settlements placed on a fairer basis. Initially, they were fighting a losing battle against the large fleet owners who could bring in workers from outside, but in March 1886, the situation was eased somewhat when the Board of Trade Inspector recommended that detailed accounts should henceforth be kept of the results of each fishing expedition, to be signed by the men if they were satisfied. Those who were not satisfied had rights of appeal.

By the time Grimsby became a County Borough (1 April 1891), its fishing industry had significantly changed. Sailing vessels were rapidly being replaced by steam so that, by the end of 1898, only 277 sailing smacks and liners were left, compared to 340 trawlers – most of which were less than six years old. Two years later, there were only sixty-one fishing smacks, but the number of trawlers had increased to 471. Annual catches landed between 1893 and 1897 respectively varied from 80,134 tons to 97,921 tons (Figure 3 and Figure 4), a large proportion of which was transported by rail throughout

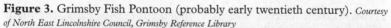

Figure 3. Grimsby Fish Pontoon (probably early twentieth century). *Courtesy of North East Lincolnshire Council, Grimsby Reference Library*

Figure 4. The Pontoon at Grimsby. *Courtesy of North East Lincolnshire Council, Grimsby Reference Library*

the whole of the country.

Share fishing was also at an end by 1901, as trawler crews were now paid under a system in which wages were supplemented by a percentage of the proceeds of the voyage. The fishermen, believing they would be worse off under this ruling, fought against the newly organised Grimsby Federated Protection Society that insisted crews could only be signed on under these new terms. The fishermen went on strike in July that same year, leaving over 400 trawlers to stand idle.

As smacks were not affected, they enjoyed a period of renewed popularity; but, for most crewmen, the times were hard. When foreigners were brought in to man the trawlers, riots broke out on the Fish Dock and the Federation offices were smashed, completely damaging the fishermen's cause. Detachments from the Sheffield and Manchester police forces, plus members of the Lincolnshire Regiment, were brought in and the *Riot Act* was read out in the town's Riby Square.

This unhappy state continued until October when the men were forced to give in and return to work on terms offered by the Federation, pending an award by an arbitrator. The reduction in wages they had fought against was imposed, and any increase in their earnings had to come from the poundage – which, it was expected, would be kept at a minimum figure by the employers' accountants. Another hundred trawlers were added to the fleet, and the smacks, now no longer needed, decreased in number to just thirty. In 1904, a figure of 483 steam trawlers was registered at Grimsby.

Figure 5. Fish cleaning, probably early twentieth century. *Courtesy of North East Lincolnshire Council, Grimsby Reference Library*

Effects of a world war

By 1913, Grimsby had a fleet of 625 trawlers, made up of 595 steam driven and thirty sailing smacks. Although approximately 100 new steam trawlers were being registered annually in Grimsby at the turn of the twentieth century, at the start of the First World War (1914), that figure was somewhat reduced. Each vessel consumed between 1,500 and 2,000 tons of coal a year, with about five tons of coal being needed to produce one ton of fish (Figure 5).

At the outbreak of the war, more than 500 trawlers were requisitioned by the Admiralty, mainly for minesweeping duties. There were many instances recorded of heroism by seamen on those battle-torn seas. For example, the *Grimsby News* reported on 27 September 1914, a month after war had broken out:

> *Presentations were made to the skippers of three Grimsby trawlers – William Holt of the* Silanion, *Henry Wicks of the* Straton *and Mark Howard of the* Prince Victor. *All directed their trawlers to the area where the Wilson liner* Runo *had been blown up. At great peril they succeeded in saving so many of the passengers and crew, that what looked like being an appalling disaster was considerably minimised. Experience had shown that where there was one mine, there was every possibility others had been laid in the same area. Gold watches and Alberts were handed to the three skippers.*

Eventually, equipment on board the trawlers was supplemented by anti-submarine bomb throwers, depth charges and hydrophones. The Admiralty also built and added about 1,000 trawler-type vessels to the fleet. The few trawlers left for fishing duties were taken over by the Admiralty in 1917, flying the White Ensign although still being run by the owners.

Between the wars

Despite a post-war recession, the fishing industry, which was under Government control for a time, quickly recovered. Surviving trawlers went back to the job for which they were made, new vessels were built and more men trained to work within the industry.

As the number of catches landed at Grimsby port continued to increase, the need to create more spacious accommodation became a great priority. In 1934, the construction of a new dock was eventually completed and Number 3 Fish Dock (Figure 6), along with its predecessors, was able to provide the necessary facilities to accommodate 506 steam trawlers, thirty-seven motor liners, twenty-eight steam and fifteen seine netters, plus numerous smaller craft. The amount of fish landed increased to 185,671 tons.

Coal fired ships gave way to oil/diesel powered trawlers and seine net vessels, whilst, at the same time, specialised ship repairing facilities appeared. The vice-chairman of the Grimsby Trawler Owners Association, Herbert Crampin, referred to the trawler fleet

Figure 6. Numbers 1 and 3 Fish Docks, 1960s. *Courtesy of ABP, Grimsby and Immingham*

of 1948 as being 300 vessels that, broadly speaking, fell into two classes, known locally as 'near water' and 'distant water' ships, plus smaller and more indefinite classes in between the two.

The distant or deep water boats were roughly half as long again as near water vessels, varying between 140 and 180 feet in length, but more than double the tonnage of their sister ships. Post-war steam vessels were capable of good speeds, more streamlined, contained more safety devices, better quarters for crews and had radio contact with other trawlers. This was some help in the trawling fleet's continual fight against the elements and the risks of men falling or being swept overboard.

Grimsby's fishermen began making three and four-week trips to Norway, Finland, Iceland, the northern coasts of Russia, Bear Island – and they even sailed as far north as Spitzbergen. Crews numbered between twenty and twenty-five, and hauls of around 250 tons were made. Back in dock, the catch was landed. In the early days of the industry, it had been displayed in large heaps for prospective buyers to view; later it was set out in wooden boxes that held an average of about ten stone of fish – except for large skate and halibut, which would be laid out in single pieces, each with its weight displayed. The next type of container came in the form of reusable aluminium boxes, which, in turn, were phased out following the introduction of plastic boxes in 1973. Nowadays, fifty kilo (eight stone) plastic containers are more commonly used. (A different type of plastic container is used by trawlers that box their catch whilst still at sea.)

Although life was hard, it was also a time when the townsfolk began to enjoy the results of their harvest from the sea. It is believed that more people owned their own homes and cars in Grimsby and its surrounding area at this time, than any other town in the country. But there was another war on the horizon.

The Second World War
As the threat of a second world war grew ever more ominous in 1939, all Grimsby ships were recalled by radio. They had to return to port by devious routes in accordance with the secret instructions all skippers had carried for months and, within a few days, most were flying the White Ensign. Of Grimsby's registered fleet of 458 vessels, 120 were deep-water boats, and once again, most were requisitioned by the Admiralty. It was mainly the small and old trawlers left for fishing duties.

When specially built minesweepers came into operation, some of the older and slower vessels were returned to the fishing fleet in order to help improve the food situation. Trawlers were also used during hostilities as rescue ships to save the lives of men from torpedoed vessels – being extremely seaworthy, fast enough to keep up with the convoys, and too small to be worthy of German torpedoes.

One hundred years of fishing

Great Grimsby's fishing industry celebrated its first one hundred years of business in 1956. It was leading the world with record figures regarding quantity, quality and turnover value of fish landed at its Port (Figure 7). Twenty-five new steam trawlers had been delivered since 1950, although there was still cause for concern regarding safety at sea as reports covering that same period claimed the loss of sixteen trawlers and seventy-six fishermen. Stories abound of acts of heroism by these seamen. One such tale was reported by the *Grimsby Evening Telegraph* on 11 December 1959:

> *...magnificent seamanship enabled the 42-year-old Grimsby trawler* War Duke *to manoeuvre alongside the stricken 'baby' trawler* Janet Helen *in the fury of a south easterly North Sea gale. In spite of the towering waves, whipped up by the wind, they were able to hold the* War Duke *long enough to allow the skipper and mate of the* Janet Helen *to jump back aboard their slowly sinking vessel for a tow rope. High tribute was paid to the seamanship of Skipper George Ireland and the crew of the* War Duke *by the five crew men of the* Janet Helen *when they returned to Grimsby. Despite all the effort made, the 'baby' trawler sank after having been towed 13 miles. This rescue took place 30 miles off Flamborough Head.*

Figure 7. Trawlers at the Fish Dock, mid-twentieth century. *Courtesy of North East Lincolnshire Council, Grimsby Reference Library*

Another Cod War

In 1952, Iceland sought to control fishing in her waters by imposing a four mile limit. British trawler owners then retaliated, banning Icelandic vessels from landing their catches at the main ports in this country, leaving Iceland to seek other venues. The Icelandic limit was extended to twelve miles in 1956, but, once again, Britain would not accept this ruling. The ensuing struggle necessitated protection for the British trawler fleet by British Naval vessels. After a mutual agreement, reached in 1961, Icelandic vessels were able to land at British ports in return for access to limits within six to twelve miles of Iceland at recognised periods of the year.

It was not all smooth sailing, however, and the uneasy truce remained for only ten years, to be broken when a change of Government took place in Iceland, in 1971. Suddenly, there was a fifty mile limit was imposed, which, it was claimed, was necessary to protect the Icelandic fish stocks – that island's main source of food and income. Warps of many British trawlers were cut by Icelandic coastguard vessels, resulting in a huge loss of both catch and gear, and the whole trip had become one of even greater danger than normal – even with the protection of British naval vessels.

A compromise was eventually reached in 1973, resulting in 139 British vessels being registered to fish in certain zones for a maximum total annual catch of 130,000 tons. Large factory trawlers were excluded. This only lasted until 1975 when the existing fifty mile limit agreement ended, by which time there had been another change of Prime Minister in Iceland. When word came out that the new limit would be as much as 200 miles, there was chaos. Iceland tried to protect what she believed to be her rights by harassing the British fleet, and there were incidents of ramming and collisions between both countries' vessels as Icelandic coastguard cutters destroyed thousands of pounds worth of British gear.

It took until May 1976 for an uneasy compromise to be reached between the respective Governments. The new agreement stated that twenty-four out of a list of ninety-three British trawlers could catch up to a quota of 50,000 tons (as compared with a previous figure of 65,000 tons) per annum in Icelandic waters and, in some parts, work up to a limit of within twenty miles of the coast. That agreement lasted for just six months, after which British trawlers had to leave Icelandic waters for good.

The North Sea and Norwegian grounds were then trawled until limits were imposed there; new ventures included trips to the south-western mackerel fishing grounds and to the western edge of the

Figure 8. Number 2 Fish Dock with DFDS Terminal in foreground. *Courtesy of ABP, Grimsby and Immingham*

continental shelf where blue whiting could be found. Generally, fish supplies were greatly reduced, resulting in fewer landings so that processors and merchants were now short of supplies; fleets were also reduced, leading to fewer people being required within the industry's allied and support trades.

All this has resulted in the size of the distant-water sector of the fishing industry to become but a fraction of what it was in the mid-twentieth century. There are fewer new grounds to be opened up, and a greater awareness of the need to ration exploitation of the oceans' existing fish stocks is further restricting the likelihood of the over-fishing of specified areas.

In 1992, Grimsby Fish Dock Enterprises was formed to regenerate the Fish Docks, thereby helping to sustain the employment of more than 27,000 individuals still dependent on the fishing industry. Number 1 Fish Market was demolished to make way for the construction of a new £15 million market and distribution centre. Here, an enclosed and insulated Market Hall with modern storage, new trawler landing areas, a transport and service area and a new quay, enable speedy and efficient handling of vessels so that fish is landed in peak condition.

Once the heart of the trawling industry, Grimsby still claims to be 'officially Britain's number one fishing port'[8] (Figure 8) even though only sixty or so trawlers sail from here compared with 650 in the early twentieth century. Today, the majority of fish handled on the new market is actually landed in Scotland and transported south by road. Competition remains severe, but, Grimsby, with its background of almost 140 years as a major fishing port, supported by its well-established, associated companies specialising in fish and fish products, have helped take the town to the forefront of the European food market.

Acknowledgement

Thanks for Garry Crossland, at the ABP Port Office, Grimsby, for his help – and for casting an eye over this chapter to ensure that the facts were correct.

Notes and References

1. www.northeastlincs.com
2. *A History of Grimsby* by Edward Gillett.
3. Steep-sided, narrow ditches.
4. *Grimsby Fishing Handbook*, published for the Grimsby Fishing Vessel Owners' Association.
5. *British Fisheries* by Thomas Alward.
6. www.northeastlincs.com
7. www.northeastlincs.com
8. www.northeastlincs.com

Bibliography

Medieval Grimsby, Growth & Decline by S H Rigby.
Trawling, The Rise and Fall of the British Trawl Fishery by Robb Robinson.

CONTRIBUTORS

PIXEL OF A COASTLINE

John Malvert was born at Rimswell in the East Riding of Yorkshire in 1937, and educated at Coalbrookdale, Shropshire. He returned to Yorkshire following National Service and qualified as a Male Nurse, a position he held until retirement this year. John has lived in Lincolnshire for the last thirty years and now resides near Market Rasen. He is a member of both Market Rasen and Lincoln Phoenix Writers' Circles and has had poems, short stories, articles and other miscellaneous writings published in a number of magazines over many years.

---

1. NORTH EAST LINCOLNSHIRE BEFORE THE IRON AGE

Edward Dickinson was born in Lichfield, Staffordshire. He studied archaeology at the Institute of Archaeology, University College London, before working on archaeological sites in England and Scotland. In 1992, Edward started working for Coventry City Council at the Herbert Art Gallery and Museum, and then, in 1996, moved to North East Lincolnshire to take up the post of Archaeologist for the council. He lives in Cleethorpes with Alison, their two children and two cats.

2. SOME NORTHERN LINCOLNSHIRE HISTORIANS

Nick Lyons taught in secondary schools from 1966 to 1997. He began part-time Adult Education work, mainly for the Workers' Educational Association, in 1970, concentrating upon local studies in North Lincolnshire, especially with groups interested in research and publication.

3. WALKING THE CLAY BANK

Richard S Clarke was born and brought up in West Norfolk in a family of agricultural labourers. Since attending Hull University, he has been a secondary school history teacher for thirty-one years, as well as being a part-time tutor for Hull University, the Workers' Educational Association and the Local Authority. Richard gained his M Phil for pioneering study into the development and pre-war impact of rural council housing, with especial reference to two local authority

areas in the East Riding, but also formulating a research model which could be applied to any part of Britain. Richard is divorced and currently lives in Barton-upon-Humber. He has recently completed an HNC in Countryside Management.

4. The Founding Legend of Grimsby

Born in Seramban, British Malaya (Malaysia) **Kevin Gracie** is a grandfather, a sculptor, writer, investigator, and research historian studying the myths, legends and folklore of Lincolnshire – specialising in the legend of Grim and Havelok. In November 1999, Kevin founded the *Grim and Havelok Association* which has been responsible for finally re-publishing Charles Whistler's novel, *Havelok the Dane*, the first classic English novel, based upon the ancient British legend, to have appeared in print (1900).

5. The Humber Keels

Karen Prescott has lived in the small village of Stainforth, Doncaster, South Yorkshire, for most of her life. She moved to Owston Ferry, North Lincolnshire in 1993 where she embarked upon a Humanities Degree course, based for the first two years at North Lindsey College in Scunthorpe and the final year at Lincoln University. Karen graduated in the millennium year with an Honours Degree in English literature and history. For her dissertation entitled, *From Keel to Coal*, she chose to write about her home village, Stainforth, as, by that time, she had returned to her native roots. Up until that time, she had never heard of a Keel, and it made her realise that what was once a huge part of our history was almost extinct and unheard of by anyone below the approximate age of forty-five.

6. THE DROWNED VALLEY:
THE DRAINAGE OF THE ANCHOLME VALLEY

A retired fire officer, **Ray Carey** has lived at South Ferriby for twenty-two years. His main interests are early waterway history and a study of the lives of the people of the Low Villages in the sixteenth and seventeenth centuries. He has published a history of Lincolnshire's only island, Read's Island, a short history of South Ferriby, and, *Saxby all Saints 1667 – A Village in Crisis*. Ray's most recently publication, *Journey to Another Land* is a 156 page in-depth study of Tudor and Stuart South Ferriby which aims to illustrate that the plethora of records about local people of this period is a largely uncharted area of English history. Similar nationwide studies, he believes, would probably lead to a rewriting of national history – particularly in the social and economic fields. A full history of man's attempts to control the River Ancholme is his current project.

7. THE CLEETHORPES PROMENADES

Alan Dowling enjoys living within a few hundred yards of the Cleethorpes seafront. After early retirement from the post of head librarian for Grimsby and Cleethorpes, he took up the position of warden of the University of Hull's adult education outpost in Grimsby. Alan has carried out extensive research into the history of Grimsby and Cleethorpes and has gained a degree in local and regional history through part-time study. His main interest is in urban history and he was awarded the degree of Doctor of Philosophy for his thesis based on the development of nineteenth century Grimsby and Cleethorpes.

8. CLEETHORPES THE SEASIDE RESORT

Joanne Mason has lived and worked in Lincolnshire most of her life. She gained a degree in tourism at the newly opened, former University of Lincolnshire and Humberside. Over the past two years, she has been researching seaside tourism in Lincolnshire as part of a European Interreg IIC programme. Joanne has recently taken up the post of Tourism and Arts Officer at Boston Borough Council.

9. LETTERS FROM A SEAMAN
12. A BRIEF LOOK AT GRIMSBY'S FISHING HERITAGE

Born in Cardiff and raised in the Aberdare Valley where she attended the County Grammar School for Girls, **Jenny Walton** is proud of her Welsh heritage. Yet, as a resident of Lincolnshire for the past thirty-seven years, she is also proud to be an 'adopted' Yellow Belly. Married, and a grandmother, Jenny has four dogs and three cats and enjoys singing, particularly West Gallery Quire music. She has worked as a writer/editor for a number of regional and national publications, and is also involved in researching and scriptwriting documentary videos.

10. SOME ASPECTS OF A PRE-ENCLOSURE FARM IN BARROW-UPON-HUMBER

Neil Robert Wilkyn was born in Lincolnshire in 1950 and educated at Caistor Grammar School. He dropped history and Latin GCE in favour of the sciences but quite soon realised his mistake. He became interested in local history via family history research and took a part time degree course through Hull University, graduating with first class honours in 1996. Neil has since written two books on local history; one on the copyhold tenants of the manor of Barrow-upon-Humber, and one detailing village life in Barnetby in the sixteenth to eighteenth centuries based on probate inventories. He now tutors regularly for the WEA in North Lincolnshire as well as working full time. Neil is married, with two grown up sons.

11. THE COASTAL AIRFIELDS OF LINCOLNSHIRE

Patrick Otter is the author of *Lincolnshire Airfields in the Second World War*. He is the son of an RAF navigator and was brought up in Gainsborough. After leaving the town's Grammar School, he worked on several newspapers in the county before joining the *Grimsby Evening Telegraph* in 1970. Patrick was to hold a number of positions with the paper before being appointed Assistant Editor in 1988, retiring on health grounds in 1997. He has had a lifelong interest in the county's airfields and is also the author of a three-volume series on 1 Group of Bomber Command and *Yorkshire Airfields in the Second World War*.